Advances in Scalable Web Information Integration and Service

Advances in Scalable Web Information Integration and Service

Proceedings of DASFAA2007 International Workshop on
Scalable Web Information Integration and Service (SWIIS2007)

Bangkok, Thailand   9 – 12 April 2007

editors

Yoshifumi Masunaga
Aoyama Gakuin University, Japan

Xiaofeng Meng
Renmin University of China, China

Guoren Wang
Northeastern University, China

Seog Park
Sogang University, Korea

World Scientific

NEW JERSEY · LONDON · SINGAPORE · BEIJING · SHANGHAI · HONG KONG · TAIPEI · CHENNAI

Published by

World Scientific Publishing Co. Pte. Ltd.

5 Toh Tuck Link, Singapore 596224

USA office: 27 Warren Street, Suite 401-402, Hackensack, NJ 07601

UK office: 57 Shelton Street, Covent Garden, London WC2H 9HE

British Library Cataloguing-in-Publication Data
A catalogue record for this book is available from the British Library.

ISBN-13 978-981-277-023-3
ISBN-10 981-277-023-2

Printed in Singapore.

Workshop Organizers

PC Co-Chairs:
- Xiaofeng Meng, Renmin University of China, China
- Guoren Wang, Northeastern University, China

Advisory Committee
- Yoshifumi Masunaga, Ochanomizu University, Japan
- Tok Wang Ling, NUS, Singapore
- Shan Wang, Renmin University of China, China
- Longxiang Zhou, Institute of Mathematics, CAS, China

Program Committee
- Lei Chen, Hong Kong University of Technology, China
- Xiaoyong Du, Renmin University of China, China
- Ling Feng, Tsinghua University, China
- Yaokai Feng, Kyushu University, Japan
- Hong Gao, Harbin Institute of Technology, China
- Yan Jia, National U. of Defence Technology, China
- Sang-goo Lee, Seoul National University, Korea
- Chen Li, University of California (Irvine), USA
- Qing Li, City University of Hong Kong, Hong Kong
- Xuemin Lin, University of New South Wales, Australia
- Mengchi Liu, Carleton University, Canada
- Jian Pei, Simon Fraser University, Canada
- Keun Ho Ryu, Chungbuk National University, Korea
- Zhiyong Peng, Wuhan University, China
- Changjie Tang, Sichuan University, China
- Botao Wang, Northeastern University, China
- Daling Wang, Northeastern University, China
- Haixun Wang, IBM Research, USA
- Tengjiao Wang, Peking University, China
- Wei Wang, Fudan University, China
- Wei Wang, University of New South Wales, Australia
- Yitong Wang, Fudan University, China
- Jirong Wen, Microsoft Research Asia, China
- Jeffrey X. Yu, Chinese University of Hong Kong
- Jian Yang, Macquarie University, Australia
- Yanchun Zhang, Victoria University, Australia
- Shuigeng Zhou, Fudan University, China

Preface

Recent advances in Web technologies and applications such as Web Data Management, Web Information Integration, Web Services, Web Data Warehousing, Web Data Mining, have rapidly changed our life in various ways. The objective of the workshop is to bring together researchers, industrial practitioners, and developers to study how the Web information can be extracted, stored, analyzed, and processed to provide useful knowledge to the end users for various advanced database and Web applications. This workshop aims to promote all the areas related to Web information technology.

This first workshop was organized in conjunction with the 12th International Conference on Database Systems for Advanced Applications (DASFAA2007), held in Bangkok, Thailand. The workshop Call for Papers (CFP) solicited contributions covering:

- Web Information Integration
- Web and XML Data Management
- P2P-based Information Management
- Web Services

- Web Mining
- Web Data Warehousing and Web Exploration
- Web 2.0 based Information Infrastructure
- Deep Web

After peer review, eight papers were selected for presentation from 18 submissions. These were grouped into three sessions: semantic web and deep web, web service, and data integration. Moreover, a special session including three invited papers was also organized.

The organizer of the workshop would like to thank all program committee members, as well as all external referees, for their excellent work in evaluating the submitted papers. We are also very grateful to the organizer of DASFAA 2007 for their help and support. Finally, our sincere thanks to Prof. Tok Wang Ling and Prof. Katsumi Tanaka for their contributions for the workshop keynotes.

Xiaofeng Meng
Guoren Wang
(Program Co-chairs)

Table of Contents

Invited Session

Session 1: Semantic Web and Deep Web

Session 2: Web Service

Session 3: Data Integration

USING SEMANTICS IN XML DATA MANAGEMENT

TOK WANG LING

Department of Computer Science, National University of Singapore, Singapore
E-mail: lingtw@comp.nus.edu.sg

GILLIAN DOBBIE

Department of Computer Science, University or Auckland, New Zealand
E-mail: gill@cs.auckland.ac.nz

XML is emerging as a de facto standard for information exchange over the Web, while businesses and enterprises generate and exchange large amounts of XML data daily. One of the major challenges is how to query this data efficiently. Queries typically can be represented as twig patterns. Some researchers have developed algorithms that reduce the intermediate results that are generated during query processing, while others have introduced labeling schemes that encode the position of elements, enabling queries to be answered by accessing the labels without traversing the original XML documents. In this paper we outline optimizations that are based on semantics of the data being queried, and introduce efficient algorithms for content and keyword searches in XML databases. If the semantics are known we can further optimize the query processing, but if the semantics are unknown we revert to the traditional query processing approaches.

Keywords: XML, query processing, query optimization, keyword search

1. Introduction

Semistructured data has become more prevalent with the increasing number of advanced applications on the Web. Many of these applications, such as electronic market places, produce and consume large volumes of data. XML (eXtended Markup Language) is emerging as the de facto standard for semistructured data on the Web. Although XML documents could have rather complex internal structures, they can generally be modeled as ordered trees.

In most XML query languages, the structures of XML queries are expressed as twig (i.e. a small tree) patterns, while the values of XML elements are used as part of the selection predicates. Efficiently matching all twig patterns in an XML database is a major concern in XML query processing. Among them, holistic twig join approaches have been accepted as an efficient way to match twig patterns, reducing the size of the intermediate result.[1] Recently many algorithms have been proposed including TwigStack,[2] TJFast,[3] TwigStackList,[4] Tag+level,[5] prefix path stream (PPS),[6] OrderedTJ.[7] They are based on a form of labeling scheme that encodes each element in an XML database using its positional information. In order to answer a query twig pattern, these algorithms access the labels alone without traversing the original XML documents.

In this paper we outline an innovative way to process XML queries that takes into account the semantics of the data, and introduce an efficient algorithm for keyword searches in XML databases. The essence of the approach is that semantics of the data can be used in query optimization if the semantics of the data are known, otherwise a more traditional approach to query processing will be adopted. Some of the semantics can be represented in schema languages such as DTD[8] and XMLSchema[9] but there is other information that can be used in query processing that cannot be represented in these schema definition languages.

Typically, XML data is simply modeled as a tree structure without the important concepts object class, attribute of object class, relationship type defined among object classes, and attribute of relationship type. We have defined a data model called ORA-SS - Object-Relationship-Attribute Model for Semistructured Data, which includes the concepts in the Entity-Relationship data model together with constructs to capture the hierarchical structure of XML data. With the ORA-SS data model, many semantics of the XML database can be explicitly represented. Semantics that can be represented in the ORA-SS data model but cannot be specified by DTD and XMLSchema include:

(1) Attribute vs. object class. Data can be represented in XML documents either as attributes or element. So, it is difficult to tell from the XML document whether a child element is in fact an attribute of its parent element or an object. DTD and XMLSchema cannot specify that a child element is an attribute of its parent element.

(2) Multivalued attribute vs. object class. In XML document, multivalued attributes of an object class have to be represented as child elements. DTD and XMLSchema cannot specify that a child element is a multivalued attribute of its parent element.

(3) Identifier (ID). DTD and XMLSchema cannot specify the identifier of an object class which appears as a child element and has a many to

many relationship with its parent element. ID and key of DTD and XMLSchema respectively, are not powerful enough to represent the identifier of such object classes.

(4) IDREF or Foreign Key. As DTD and XMLSchema cannot represent identifiers of some object classes, so foreign key or ID reference of such object classes cannot be specified.

(5) N-ary relationship type. DTD and XMLSchema can only specify child elements of a parent element, such a relationship is the parent-child relationship and it is a binary relationship type. Ternary relationship types and N-ary relationship types among object classes cannot be specified by DTD and XMLSchema.

(6) Attribute of object class vs. attribute of relationship type. As DTD and XMLSchema do not have the concept of object classes and relationship types (they only represent the hierarchical structure of elements and attributes), there is no way to specify whether an attribute of a element is an attribute of the element (object class) or an attribute of some relationship type involving the element (object class) and its ancestors (object classes).

(7) View of XML document. Since DTD and XMLSchema cannot specify identifiers and attributes of object classes and relationship types, DTD and XMLSchema do not contain semantics to define views of XML document which change the hierarchical order of object classes (elements) in the original XML document.

The above semantics (1 to 6) can be captured in the ORA-SS schema diagram, and because of these semantics, we can define a valid XML view which changes the hierarchical order of object classes using a swap operator.[10] With the semantics captured in the ORA-SS schema diagram of an XML database, twig pattern queries on the XML database can be optimized significantly. Using the work we have done with views, we can guarantee that if a query changes the hierarchical order of nodes, the semantics of the output is consistent with the semantics of the XML document. DTD and XMLSchema cannot be used to interpret the output part when the hierarchical ordering of nodes in the output is different than in the query part. With the semantics captured by the ORA-SS data model, we will be able to interpret XML queries correctly and improve the query evaluation performance using these semantics.

In the rest of the paper, we briefly review related work in XML query processing in Section 2, and use an example to introduce the key concepts of the ORA-SS data model in Section 3. In Section 4 we outline how the semantics represented in the ORA-SS data model can improve the speed of query processing. In Section 6 we introduce an efficient algorithm for keyword searches in XML databases and we conclude in Section 7.

2. Related Work

XPath[11] is a language for finding information in an XML document by navigating through elements and attributes in an XML document. Its syntax is similar to directories in UNIX file systems. For example, find the names of the students taking the course "cs4221" can be expressed by the XPath expression:

/department/course[code= "cs4221"]/student/stuName

An XPath query can be expressed graphically by a small tree called a twig pattern. The above XPath query is represented as the twig pattern query shown in Figure 1.

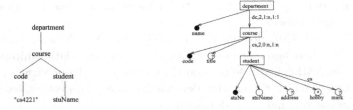

Fig. 1. Example Twig Pattern Query   Fig. 2. ORA-SS Schema Diagram

Twig join processing is central to XML query evaluation. Extensive research efforts have been put into efficient twig pattern query processing with label based structural joins. Zhang et al.[12] first proposed multi-predicate merge join (MPMGJN) based on containment labeling of XML documents. The later work by Al-Khalifa et al.[13] proposed an improved stack-based structural join algorithm, called Stack-Tree-Desc/Anc. Both of these are binary structural joins and may produce large amounts of useless intermediate results. Bruno et al.[2] then proposed a holistic twig join algorithm, called TwigStack, to address and solve the problem of useless intermediate results. However, TwigStack is only optimal in terms of intermediate results for twig queries with only ancestor-descendent relationships. It has been proven that optimal evaluation of twig patterns with arbitrarily mixed ancestor-descendent and parent-child relationships is not feasible.[14] There are many subsequent works that optimize TwigStack in terms of I/O, or extend TwigStack for different problems.[4,5,7,15–17] In particular, a list structure is introduced in TwigStackList[18] for a wider range of optimizations, and TSGeneric[1] is based on indexing each stream and skipping labels within one stream. These approaches describe how to execute a query more efficiently but do not address how the semantics of the data can be used in query optimization.

Chippimolchai et al.[19] developed a semantic query optimization framework in a deductive database setting. They outline an algorithm that transforms a query to an equivalent reduced form with the introduction of integrity constraints. Queries and integrity constraints are represented as clauses and the integrity constraints are derived from the real world. They cannot be derived from XMLSchema or DTDs.

3. The ORA-SS Data Model

The Object, Relationship, Attribute data model for Semistructured Data (ORA-SS)[20] has four basic concepts: object classes, relationship types, attributes and references, and consists of four diagrams: schema diagram, instance diagram, functional dependency diagram and inheritance diagram. In this paper we are concerned with the ORA-SS schema diagram.

An ORA-SS *schema* diagram represents an object class as a labeled rectangle. A relationship type between object classes is described by a label "name (object class list), n, p, c", where *name* denotes the name of the relationship type, *object class list* is the list of objects participating in the relationship type, n is an integer indicating the degree of the relationship type, p and c are the participation constraints of the object classes in the relationship type, defined using the standard min:max notation. The edge between two object classes can have more than one such relationship type label to indicate the different relationship types the object classes participate in. Attributes of object classes or relationship types are denoted by labeled circles. Identifiers of object classes are denoted as filled circles. All attributes are assumed to be mandatory and single-valued, unless the circle contains a "?" indicating that it is single-valued and optional, or a "+" indicating that it is multivalued and required, or an "*" indicating that it is optional and multivalued. Attributes of an object class can be distinguished from attributes of a relationship type. The former has no label on its incoming edge while the latter has the name of the relationship type to which it belongs on its incoming edge.

Figure 2 shows an ORA-SS schema diagram. The rectangles labeled *department*, *course*, and *student* are the object classes. Attributes *name*,

code and *stuNo* are the identifiers of the object class *department, course*
and *student* respectively. Each *student* has a unique *stuNo*. The attributes
title, mark, address and *hobby* are optional. Attribute *hobby* is multivalued,
while *stuName* is required. There are two relationship types, called *dc*
and *cs*. The former is a binary relationship type between object classes
department and *course*, while the latter a binary relationship type between
course and *student*. A *department* can have one or more (1:n) *courses*, and
a *course* belongs to one and only one (1:1) *department*. A *course* can have
zero or more (0:n) *students*, and a *student* can take 1 or more *courses*.
The label *cs* on the edge between *student* and *mark* indicates that *mark* is
a single valued attribute of the relationship type *cs*. That is, the attribute
mark is an attribute of a *student* in a *course*. From these constraints, we
can derive that $\{course, student\} \rightarrow mark$.

4. Using Semantics in Query Processing

Here we outline how the semantics captured by ORA-SS schema can be
used to optimize twig pattern query evaluation with three twig pattern
queries. The queries refer to the schema shown in Figure 2.

Query 1: Find the stuName values of student elements having stuNo value
equals to "s123". The XPath expression is:

　　//student[@stuNo="s123"]/stuName

Using the ORA-SS schema in Figure 2, we know that stuName is a single valued attribute of the student object class and stuNo is the identifier
of the student, so $stuNo \rightarrow stuName$. To prcess the query, we only need to
find the first student element in the XML document with attribute stuNo
equal to "s123", and then find the value of its subelement stuName. However, if we use a DTD or XMLSchema of the XML data, we would not
know that stuNo is the identifier of student or that stuName is a single
valued attribute of student, so we would need to traverse the whole XML
document.

　　Additionally Wu et al.[21] have proposed an algorithm that concentrates
on searching for content or values with semantic information as compared
to structure-focused query processing. We will discuss content search in
more details in Section 5.

Query 2: Find the average marks of all the students.

To answer this query the processor needs to know that stuNo is the identifier of object class student, and mark is a single valued attribute of the relationship type between course and student. In fact, any person that writes this query in XQuery needs to use the same semantics to express the query:

for $sNo in distinct_values(//student/@stuNo)
let $mark_set := //course/student[@stuNo = $sNo]/mark
return
    <student stuNo = $sNo >
        <averagemark>{ avg($mark_set) }</averagemark>
    </student>

However, a DTD cannot express the semantics that stuNo is the identifier of student object, and also cannot express that mark is a single valued attribute of the relationship between student and course, that is {*course, student*} → *mark*. Without this information, there is no way to know whether the XQuery query with an aggregation function (or twig pattern query) is written correctly or not.

Query 3: For each student, find all courses taken by the student with the marks the student achieved in the course. Consider for example the query

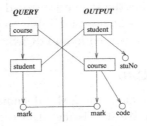

Fig. 3. Example Query Format

shown in Figure 3, where a rectangle represents an object class and a circle represents an attribute. On the left hand side the query is specified, and on the right hand side the output format is given. The lines between the query part and the output part show the correspondences between the objects in the query and those in the output. The query is asking for the marks of students in courses and in the output courses must be nested within student rather than students within courses. This query can be written in XQuery as:

```
for $sNo in distinct_values(//student/@stuNo)
let $c := //course[student/@stuNo=$sNo]
return
  <student stuNo = $sNo >
    <course code = $c/@code >
      $c/student[@stuNo=$sNo]/mark
    </course>
  </student>
```

In order to write the query above correctly, users have to know that stuNo is the identifier of student, code is the identifier of course, mark is a single valued attribute of the relationship type between course and student, each course is offered by only one department, and each course only appears once in the XML document. This information can be captured in the ORA-SS schema diagram, while DTDs and XMLSchema cannot capture all the necessary semantics.

With the semantics captured by the ORA-SS data model, we will be able to interpret whether XML queries are correct and improve the query evaluation performance using these semantics. The graphical query language GLASS[22,23] can automatically generate the XQuery for the query represented in Figure 3 using the semantics stored in the ORA-SS schema diagram in Figure 2. There is no need for a user to write XQuery queries if the semantics of the data are stored in an ORA-SS schema diagram.

5. Content Search in XML

Processing a twig pattern query in XML document includes structural search and content search. Most existing algorithms do not differentiate content search from structural search. They treat content nodes the same as element nodes during query processing with structural joins. Due to the high variety of contents, to mix content search and structure search suffers from management problem of contents and low performance. Another disadvantage is to find the actual values asked by a query, they have to rely on the original document. Therefore, we propose a novel algorithm *Value Extraction with Relational Table (VERT)* to overcome these limitations.[21] The main technique of *VERT* is introducing relational tables to store document contents instead of treating them as nodes and labeling them. Tables in our algorithm are created based on semantic information of documents. As more semantics captured, we can further optimize tables and queries to significantly enhance efficiency.

For example, consider the example XML tree with containment labels in Figure 4. Instead of storing the label streams for each XML tag and value contents, we can store the value contents together with the labels of their parent tags in relational tables as shown in Figure 5. With these relational tables, when a user issues a twig query as shown in Figure 6(a), the system can automatically rewrite it to the query shown in Figure 6(b), where the node price, the value node with value greater than 15, and their PC relationship are replaced by a node called $price'_{>15}$. Then, we can execute SQL in table R_{price} to get all labels of $price$ elements with value greater than 15 to form the label stream for $price'_{>15}$; and perform structural join based on label streams of $book$, $ISBN$ and $price'_{>15}$. In this way, we save both the stream merge cost of all content values greater than 15 and the structural join between the merged label streams for content values and $price$ element.

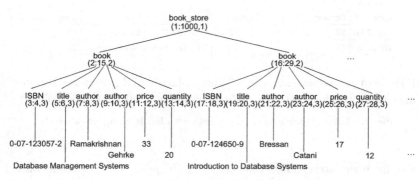

Fig. 4.   Example labeled XML tree

R_{ISBN}

Label	Content
(3:4,3)	0-07-123057-2
(17:18,3)	0-07-124650-9
...	...

R_{title}

Label	Content
(5:6,3)	Database Management Systems
(19:20,3)	Introduction to Database Systems
...	...

R_{price}

Label	Content
(11:12,3)	33
(25:26,3)	17
...	...

Fig. 5.   Some example tables to store contents with their parent labels

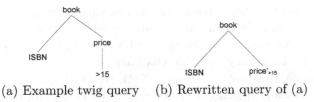

(a) Example twig query   (b) Rewritten query of (a)

Fig. 6.   Example twig patten queries and its rewritten query

Moreover, if we know that *price* is a property of *book* object class by exploiting the schema information, we can directly put the value contents of *price* with labels of *book* object class, instead of the labels of *price* element, as shown in Figure 7(a). In this way, when processing the twig query in Figure 6, we can also save the structural join between *book* object and its *price* property. Note that we can also store the labels of *book* objects with the contents of other properties, such as *title*, *author*, etc., which are not shown due to limited space.

$R_{book/price}$

Label	Content
(11:12,3)	33
(25:26,3)	17
...	...

R_{book}

Label	ISBN	title	price	quantity
(11:12,3)	0-07-123057-2	Database ...	33	20
(25:26,3)	0-07-124650-9	Introduction ...	17	12
...	...	...	...	...

(a) Table of *price* contents and *book* object labels   (b) Table of labels and pre-merged single-valued property contents of *book* object

Fig. 7.   Example table to store contents with labels of object classes

Finally, if we further know that *ISBN*, *title*, *price*, etc. are single-valued properties of *book* object class according to semantics captured by ORA-SS, we can pre-merge the content values of these properties into a single relational table with the labels of *book* objects as shown in Figure 7(b). With the pre-merged table, to answer the twig query in Figure 6, we can simply perform an efficient selection on the pre-merged table without time consuming structural joins. Note that we should not merge multi-valued properties (e.g. *author*) into the table to avoid duplicate information.

Experimental evaluation shows that besides solving different content problems, *VERT* also has superiority in performance of twig pattern query processing comparing with existing algorithms.

6. Keyword Search with Semantics in XML

Keyword proximity search is a user-friendly way to query XML databases. Most previous efforts in this area focus on keyword proximity search in XML based on either a tree data model or a graph (or digraph) data model. Tree data models for XML are generally simple and efficient. However, they do not capture connections such as ID references in XML databases. In contrast, techniques based on a graph (or digraph) model capture connections, but are generally inefficient to compute. Moreover, most of the existing techniques do not exploit schema information which is usually present in XML databases. Without schema information, keyword proximity techniques may have difficulty in presenting results, and more importantly, they return many irrelevant results. For example, the LCA (Lowest Common Ancestor) semantics for keyword proximity search based on tree model may return the overwhelmingly large root of the whole XML database.

Therefore, we propose an interconnected object model to fully exploit the property of XML and the underlining schema information when the schema is present.[24] In our model, database administrators identify interested object classes for result display and the conceptual connections between interested objects. For example, the interested object trees in DBLP can be publications; and the conceptual connection between publications can be reference and citation relationships.

With interested object classes, the most intuitive result of keyword proximity search is a list of interested objects containing all keywords. We call these interested objects as ICA (Interested Common Ancestor) in contrast to the well-known LCA (Lowest Common Ancestor) semantics. Also, and more importantly, we propose IRA (Interested Related Ancestors) semantics to capture conceptual connections between interested objects and include more relevant results that do not contain all keywords. An IRA result is a pair of objects that together contain all keywords and are connected by conceptual connections. An object is an IRA object if it belongs to some IRA pair. For example, for query "XML query processing", the paper with title "query processing" and citing or cited by "XML" papers are considered as IRA objects. Further, we propose RelevanceRank to rank IRA objects according to their relevance scores to the query. RelevanceRank is application dependent. For an intuitive example, in DBLP, for query "XML query processing", a "query processing" paper that cites or is cited by many "XML" papers is ranked higher than another "query processing" paper that cites or is cited by only one "XML" papers. Other ranking metrics can also be incorporated with RelevanceRank. For example, for query

"John Smith", we can use proximity rank to rank papers with author "John Smith" higher than papers with co-author "John" and "Smith".

Experimental evaluation shows our approach is superior to most existing academic systems in terms of execution time and result quality. Our approach is also superior or comparable to commercial systems such as Google Scholar and Microsoft Libra in term of result quality.

7. Conclusion

One of the important areas in the management of semistructured data is providing algorithms that enable efficient querying of the data. Many researchers have investigated matching twig patterns, using clever matching algorithms and included labeling schemes which enable smart ways of determining the relationships between nodes in a tree, without traversing the tree.

In this paper, we outline some optimizations that can be introduced when semantics of the data are known. We introduce a data model, ORA-SS in which the necessary semantics can be represented, and describe the kinds of optimizations that can be done. We demonstrate how twig patterns can be optimized when semantics are included, how to process values in holistic twig join algorithms, and how conceptual connections between object classes can be used in keyword proximity searches.

In the future we will study how to use other semantics captured in ORA-SS schema diagrams to further optimize the evaluation of twig pattern queries, provide guidelines of where these optimizations are worthwhile, and show the improvement in processing speed through experimentation. The particular areas we will look at include how specific information in twig queries interact with optimization such as parent-child and ancestor-descendant relationships, negation, ordering of nodes, constant values, and output nodes.[22]

References

1. H. Jiang, W. Wang, H. Lu and J. X. Yu, Holistic twig joins on indexed XML documents, in *VLDB*, 2003.
2. N. Bruno, N. Koudas and D. Srivastava, Holistic twig joins: optimal XML pattern matching, in *SIGMOD Conference*, 2002.
3. J. Lu, T. Chen and T. W. Ling, TJFast: effective processing of XML twig pattern matching, in *WWW (Special interest tracks and posters)*, 2005.
4. T. Yu, T. W. Ling and J. Lu, TwigStackList: A holistic twig join algorithm for twig query with not-predicates on XML data, in *DASFAA*, 2006.

5. T. Chen, J. Lu and T. W. Ling, On boosting holism in XML twig pattern matching using structural indexing techniques, in *SIGMOD Conference*, 2005.

6. T. Chen, T. W. Ling and C. Y. Chan, Prefix path streaming: A new clustering method for optimal holistic XML twig pattern matching, in *DEXA*, 2004.

7. J. Lu, T. W. Ling, C. Y. Chan and T. Chen, From region encoding to extended dewey: On efficient processing of XML twig pattern matching, in *VLDB*, 2005.

8. T. Bray, J. Paoli and C. M. Sperberg-McQueen, Extensible markup language (XML) 1.0. 2nd edition http://www.w3.org/TR/REC-xml, (Oct. 2000).

9. H. Thompson, D. Beech, M. Maloney and N. M. (Eds), XML Schema Part 1: Structures http://www.w3.org/TR/xmlschema-1, (May 2001).

10. Y. B. Chen, T. W. Ling and M.-L. Lee, Designing valid XML views, in *ER*, 2002.

11. J. Clark and S. DeRose, XMLpath language XPath version 1.0 http://www.w3.org/TR/xpath, (Nov. 1999).

12. C. Zhang, J. F. Naughton, D. J. DeWitt, Q. Luo and G. M. Lohman, On supporting containment queries in relational database management systems, in *SIGMOD Conference*, 2001.

13. S. Al-Khalifa, H. V. Jagadish, J. M. Patel, Y. Wu, N. Koudas and D. Srivastava, Structural joins: A primitive for efficient XML query pattern matching, in *ICDE*, 2002.

14. B. Choi, M. Mahoui and D. Wood, On the optimality of holistic algorithms for twig queries, in *DEXA*, 2003.

15. H. Jiang, H. Lu and W. Wang, Efficient processing of twig queries with or-predicates, in *SIGMOD Conference*, 2004.

16. J. Lu, T. W. Ling, T. Yu, C. Li and W. Ni, Efficient processing of ordered XML twig pattern, in *DEXA*, 2005.

17. B. Chen, T. W. Ling, T. Ozsu and Z. Zhu, *To appear in DASFAA 2007*.

18. J. Lu, T. Chen and T. W. Ling, Efficient processing of XML twig patterns with parent child edges: a look-ahead approach, in *CIKM*, 2004.

19. P. Chippimolchai, V. Wuwongse and C. Anutariya, Towards semantic query optimization for XML databases, in *ICDE Workshops*, 2005.

20. T. W. Ling, M. L. Lee and G. Dobbie, *Semistructured database design* (Springer, 2005).

21. H. Wu, T. W. Ling and B. Chen, VERT: an efficient algorithm for content search and content extraction in XML query processing. Submitted for publication.

22. W. Ni and T. W. Ling, GLASS: A graphical query language for semistructured data, in *DASFAA*, 2003.

23. W. Ni and T. W. Ling, Translate graphical XML query language to SQLX, in *DASFAA*, 2005.

24. B. Chen, J. Lu and T. W. Ling, LCRA: effective semantics for XML keyword search. Submitted for publication.

PROCESSING WEB AGGREGATE QUERIES BY ANALYZING SEARCH ENGINE INDICES

SATOSHI OYAMA, TARO TEZUKA, HIROAKI OHSHIMA

and KATSUMI TANAKA

Graduate School of Informatics, Kyoto University,
Kyoto 606-8501, Japan
E-mail: {oyama,tezuka,ohshima,tanaka}@dl.kuis.kyoto-u.ac.jp

We propose a method for processing aggregate queries by analyzing indices of Web search engines. An aggregate query is a form of query such as "What are typical topics on Kyoto?" and the answer is a set of pairs of a topic term and its statistical score. Using search engine indices to process aggregate queries has two advantages. One is that we can realize quick and instant processing by using indices and minimizing the access to actual contents. The other is that results are statistically reliable since they are based on a huge amount of Web data. Our method consists of two phases. The probe phase returns a set of terms that satisfy a certain relation to a given keyword. The validation phase determines whether given terms satisfy a certain relation. We describe examples of aggregate queries: finding typical topics, finding siblings/rivals, and finding landmarks.

Keywords: Web search; Aggregate query; Query processing.

1. Introduction

Current Web search engines generally receive keywords as a query from a user and then they process the query using a keyword index and return a set of URLs of Web pages including the keywords. This type of query processing is very suitable for user needs such as "find the home page of Kyoto University," for which we can represent the query by a few keywords, for example "Kyoto University home page."

However, there is a wide variety of user information needs and many of them cannot be represented by a few keywords. Present users use Web search engines not only to find specific information (e.g., how to contact persons or organizations, bus schedules or maps), but also for surveying, comparison, and decision making. In such cases, users usually do not already have specific knowledge (the name of search targets or whether they exist). For example, a person who does not know much about Kyoto may use queries like "Find Web pages with typical topics on Kyoto or famous landmarks in it," or "Find Web pages that describe relation comparisons of Kyoto to other cities," but representing these queries through keywords is difficult.

The difficulty of representing this type of query by keywords arises because the query assumes that keywords unknown at query input time exist in the result pages. For example "typical topics" or "comparative cities" are not determined at query time, thus it is impossible for users to specify these keywords in the query.

Enabling these queries requires collecting a set of keywords that are not included in the user specified query but satisfy a certain condition like "typical topics in Kyoto." In addition, since such a query includes a qualitative condition like "typical," it is necessary to evaluate the results using some score (e.g., to measure *typicalness*) and rank or filter them. Therefore, query processing to return a set of pairs of term and corresponding score is needed. To calculate scores, some statistics about terms are required.

This type of query is similar to aggregate queries in relational databases. When processing aggregate queries, we first determine which groups of records satisfy the given conditions and then calculate statistical values, such as the frequency or average for each group. We propose the name *Web aggregate query* for the type of query introduced so far. When processing Web aggregate queries, we find terms that satisfy certain conditions and calculate statistical values for them.

We propose using Web search engine indices to process Web aggregate queries. The original purpose of the indices of Web search engines is to enable Web pages to be quickly found, but we can derive various kinds of statistical information from them. For example, the frequencies of words and phrases being used in the Web are easily determined by accessing the index. One advantage of using search engine indices to process Web aggregate queries is that it enables a quick response to queries by reducing the time-consuming access to the original contents (Web pages). The other advantage is that the indices are based on a huge amount of Web contents and they can provide statistically reliable scores. Usually, top N retrieved pages of a search engine give very biased statistical estimates because of search engines' ranking policies. On the other hand, analysis of the indices to a huge number of pages enables us to obtain less biased estimates.

In many cases, obtaining statistical information from search engine indices is easy: just send queries to the search engines.[1] Current search engines provide various search functions, such as an option to specify the positions (in title or in text) of keywords in a page or phrase search. Some search engines provide an interface through Web services, such as Google Web APIs (http://www.google.com/apis/) or Yahoo! Web Services (http://developer.yahoo.com/). Using these Web services, a program to obtain statistical information can be easily implemented.

2. A Two-phase Method for Processing Web Aggregate Queries

2.1. *Probe phase*

The probe phase receives user input keyword x and returns the set of terms $\{y_i\}$, in which each y_i satisfies some relation to x, $R(x, y_i)$. An example of such a relation is the *coordinate* relation between terms. In some cases, each term y_i is accompanied by some score s_i that represents the strength of the relation. This phase is summarized as $T = \text{Probe}(x)$, where $T = \{(y_i, s_i)|i = 1, 2, \ldots\}$ is a set of term-score pairs.

To obtain candidate terms $\{y_i\}$, the probe phase usually submits queries to a search engine and collects sample pages or snippets from them. Many search engines limit the maximum number (typically 1000) of search results that can be viewed by a user for each query. Downloading and analyzing a web page is time-consuming and this also limits the number of examples obtained in practice. Therefore, the score values obtained in this phase are usually not statistically reliable.

2.2. *Validation phase*

This phase finalizes the score for each result returned by the probe phase. That is, in this phase a pair of user input x and candidate y is received and the score is returned as $s = \text{Validation}(x, y)$. The score takes a high value if the possibility of x and y establishing the relation $R(x, y)$ appears to be high. Usually, results with scores higher than a certain threshold are selected as final results and sorted according to the score values.

3. Composing Probe and Validation Phases

3.1. *Access to search engine indices*

First, we introduce a function to obtain a set of Web pages. For example, a function to obtain N Web pages that include keyword x is $S = \text{GetPages}(x, N)$. Here, S denotes a set of Web pages. In reality, the function is composed of two steps: (1) Submit a query x to a search engine and obtain result URLs. (2) Download a web page for each URL.

The time required to process this function depends on the number of times the search engine and other Web servers are accessed. The first step does not take much time since we can get several (say, 100) URLs for each access to the search engine. However, the second phase takes longer. For each URL, it requires an access to the Web server with the URL. Therefore, we sometimes use snippets (short summaries of Web pages) returned by a search engine without downloading the actual web pages: $S = \text{GetSnippets}(x, N)$. Here, S means a set of snippets. As for URLs, many snippets can be obtained through a single access to a search engine, and access to other Web servers is not necessary.

In the validation step, the frequencies of word or phrase use in the Web are commonly applied. The function for obtaining the number of Web pages containing keyword x is $n = \text{CountPages}(x)$, where n is an integer representing the number of web pages. Actually, this function is implemented by sending only one query x to a search engine and obtaining the number search results.

3.2. Search with document structures/ linguistic patterns

Some search engines provide search options to specify the position of keywords in the structure of Web pages. If we put an option "intitle:" just before the keyword x in a Google search, it returns the URLs of pages with keyword x in the page title. Using this option, we can obtain pages with x in the title: $S = \text{GetPages}(\text{intitle}(x), N)$.

Putting a keyword in a phrase limits the meaning or role of the keyword. For example, a postpositional article ya in Japanese (that approximately corresponds to or in English) is used to introduce examples. If we want to find Web pages that include x in this pattern, we compose a phrase by adding ya just after x and use the phrase as input for the GetPages function, $S = \text{GetPages}(x + ya)$, where $+$ means concatenation of strings.

3.3. Aggregation

After obtaining a set of Web pages or snippets, the next step is to extract candidate terms from the set. Furthermore, we want to calculate statistical information to accompany each term; for example, the number of Web pages including the term among the collected Web pages. For example, a function call to obtain a set T of pairs of a noun and its frequency from a set S of Web pages or snippets is $T = \text{SelectCount}(S, \text{Noun})$. This is similar to the `select count(*)` $\cdots$ `group by` $\cdots$ statement in SQL. This function is implemented through text processing or shallow natural language processing.

In some cases we want to specify the syntactic pattern in which the term to be extracted should appear. For example, in many cases, the two terms preceding and following ya in Japanese are examples of the same category. To find terms following the given keyword x and ya and calculate their frequencies, we use the following function call: $T = \text{SelectCount}(S, \text{Noun}, \text{Following}, x + ya)$.

3.4. *Filtering*

Given two sets of term-score pairs, we can calculate the intersection of the two sets. There are several ways to calculate the new score for a term in the intersection from the scores in the original sets T_1 and T_2. If we take the geometric mean of the two scores, we use $T_3 = \text{Intersection}(T_1, T_2, \text{GeometricMean})$.

Terms with scores higher than the given threshold will be kept in the results. To select these terms, we use the function $T_2 = \text{SelectByScore}(T_1, \theta)$. Here, θ is the threshold for filtering.

4. Web Aggregate Queries

In the following, we present three examples of Web aggregate queries and show that these queries can be implemented by composing functions defined in the previous section.

4.1. *Finding typical topics*

The objective of this aggregate query is to present terms indicating typical topics for the keyword given by the user. With this query, the user can do an exploratory search for Web pages on an unfamiliar topic. For example, a traveler who plans to visit Kyoto for the first time may not know many keywords relating to topics concerning that city. Our main idea is to use the document structure of Web pages for processing this type of query.[2] Given a set of Web pages with keyword x in each title, if we find term y frequently appears in the body of the text, we can assume term y represents a typical topic relating to keyword x.

Several methods can be used to find candidate terms for typical topics for user input keyword x. One is to collect N Web pages with keyword x

in the title and select terms which appear in the page set more frequently than a threshold. This method can be written in the following pseudo-code: SelectByScore(SelectCount(GetPages(intitle(x), N), Noun), θ).

We can estimate $p(y_i|\text{intitle}(x))$, the probability of term y_i appearing in a page with keyword x in the page title. Let N be the number of collected Web pages and s_i be the number of Web pages that include term y_i; the estimation can be done as: $p(y_i|\text{intitle}(x)) \simeq \frac{s_i}{N}$.

However, this estimation may not be accurate enough since the value of N is at most 1000 and the sample size may be too small. The estimation can be done more accurately by submitting only two queries to a search engine:

$$p(y_i|\text{intitle}(x)) \simeq \frac{\text{CountPages}(\text{intitle}(x) \wedge y_i)}{\text{CountPages}(\text{intitle}(x))} \quad . \tag{1}$$

For many terms, the order of the numerator and the denominator on the right side of this equation exceeds 10^4, so we can obtain a more reliable estimate of the probability. A concern is that very general words, such as "page" or "information," have high probability according to (1) regardless of x. To eliminate these words from the candidates, we also estimate the ordinal co-occurrence probability without considering the positions of terms in a page, and compare the probability considering positions. We keep y_i in the results only if it satisfies the following condition: $p(y_i|\text{intitle}(x)) \gg p(y_i|x)$.

To measure the statistical significance of the differences between the two probabilities, we can use the χ^2 score, which can be estimated from the number of search results provided by a search engine.[2]

Table 1 shows terms found for typical topics for a given keyword "Thailand." In the probe phase, 50 Web pages with the keyword were collected. These experiments were done in Japanese and the results translated into English. Single characters seemingly due to errors in the Japanese morphological analysis were removed from the table. Famous sightseeing places such as Bangkok and Chiang Mai, and common interests of visitors, such as the currency and language, are listed in the results.

4.2. *Finding siblings/rivals*

The objective of this aggregate query is to discover terms which indicate siblings/rivals of a query keyword. We call such terms *coordinate terms*. Coordinate terms are terms which share the same hypernym of the given query keyword. For example, "Kyoto University" and "Osaka University"

Table 1. Topic terms for Thailand.

Topic term	$p(y_i|\text{intitle}(x))$	$p(y_i|x)$	χ^2
Bangkok	0.321	0.080	1007301.19
Chiang Mai	0.137	0.020	894913.74
Thai	0.153	0.027	770004.15
Baht	0.126	0.020	743802.37
Thailand	0.113	0.017	682850.79
Thai language	0.158	0.033	615831.80
Domestic Thailand	0.058	0.007	462268.37
Phuket	0.099	0.019	438914.32
In Thailand	0.052	0.006	405510.61
Pattaya	0.054	0.009	291393.31
Thai Kingdom	0.058	0.011	255938.42
Ayutthaya	0.047	0.008	237752.17

are coordinate terms to each other because they have the same hypernym, "university."

Finding coordinate terms is necessary (and otherwise useful) in the case of a user who wants to compare a certain thing to something, but does not know the comparable things. Two assumptions are made to find coordinate terms.[3] The first is that two coordinate terms can be connected with a coordinating conjunction which functions like an *or* condition. In Japanese, the conjunction *ya* has the same meaning as *or*, so we use *ya* as the representation of a coordinating conjunction. The second assumption is that if term x and term y are truly coordinate terms, both the $x + ya + y$ pattern and the $y + ya + x$ pattern must frequently appear.

In the first phase, we find coordinate-term candidates for a given query keyword. Terms which are connected to the query keyword with a coordinating conjunction *ya* can be treated as candidates. There are several ways to find such terms; one is to use snippets of Web search results. This is represented as $\text{SelectByScore}(T, \theta)$, where

$T = \text{Intersection}($

$\quad \text{SelectCount}(\text{GetSnippets}(x + ya), \text{Noun}, \text{Following}, x + ya),$

$\quad \text{SelectCount}(\text{GetSnippets}(ya + x), \text{Noun}, \text{Preceding}, ya + x),$

$\quad \text{GeometricMean})\ .$

The validation formula is

$$p(\text{connected}(x, y)|\text{cooccurrent}(x, y))$$
$$\simeq \frac{\text{CountPages}((x + ya + y) \vee (y + ya + x))}{\text{CountPages}(x \wedge y)},$$

Table 2.   Examples from the validation phase.

Kyoto University		Oracle	
Term	Probability	Term	Probability
University of Tokyo	3.50E-04	SQL Server	3.91E-04
Osaka University	2.07E-04	SAP	1.74E-05
Tokyo	3.15E-05	information	5.68E-06
University	3.58E-06	OS	1.03E-06
information	9.04E-09	Database	3.12E-08

which represents the conditional probability that x and y are *connected* with the coordinate conjunction if they *co-occur*, and it can be used to estimate the *coordinateness* of two words.

Table 2 shows examples of results from the validation phase. When the query was Kyoto University, the University of Tokyo and Osaka University were relevant coordinate terms, but the others were irrelevant. The validation value obviously becomes larger when a candidate term is relevant. In the other example, where the query was Oracle, SQL Server was a rival as a database management system and SAP was a rival as a company. The context was different for each, but the validation method worked well.

4.3. *Finding Landmarks*

In this aggregate query, our goal is to extract landmarks, which are cognitively significant objects on a geographic scale. In our approach, landmarks are extracted out of a list of place names in a conventional geographical information system (GIS). While the names and coordinates of geographic objects are usually available through a GIS, their levels of cognitive significance are often unavailable. Analyzing Web search engine indices provides a way to obtain landmark information. The underlying assumption is that the usage of a place name on the Web reflects its significance in people's minds.[4]

For this aggregate query, the probe phase collects place names y_i from a GIS. In the validation phase, we rank place names by sending queries to search engines. One possible measurement for ranking is by document frequency (DF) of place names in the Web. We can estimate this value from the results of the search engines: CountPages(y_i). The result often contains considerable noise, though, due to the ambiguities of place names. For example, McDonald's and Virgin Records are highly ranked if they are contained in a GIS, but they are not necessarily landmarks. It is important for a map interface to present place names that have significant spatial roles, rather than those with general significance. Document frequencies do not reflect such significance directly.

To cope with this problem, we add a grammatical element to a place name. According to the case structure grammar, a deep case or a thematic role is a fundamental attribute that each noun phrase has in relation to the predicate.[5] A grammatical element, or a surface case, is an explicit indicator of a deep case. In Japanese, a spatial case particle indicates a surface case, meaning that the noun phrase is used to specify a location, a source, or a goal. Examples of common spatial case particles in Japanese are *de* (at/on/in), *kara* (from), *made* (to), *e* (to), *ni* (to). If a place name y_i is frequently used with these case particles, then we can assume that it has a spatial significance. Formerly, this is expressed as CountPages($y_i + (de \lor kara \lor made \lor e \lor ni)$) .

The result is a spatial case frequency (SCF), indicating how often a place name is used in a spatial sense. By adding these grammatical elements to the search query, the system ranks place names in order of estimated spatial significance. The output still contains many erroneous rankings. One problem is that many place names are used to indicate different locations and SCF is vulnerable to ambiguities in place names. To obtain an appropriate list of landmarks, the system must check co-occurrences with the region name to ensure each one is significant in the area.

We performed an experiment on the extraction of landmarks from place names in Kyoto, Japan. 257 place names, consisting of stations, universities, temples, and natural features were ranked according to their frequencies when attached with spatial case particles. Table 3 shows a list of the place names with the highest SCF values obtained during the validation phase. The intermediate results show high precision, but a noticeable error is that Kasuga Shrine, ranked 15th, is probably ranked too high due to ambiguity. The most famous Kasuga Shrine is in nearby Nara, and the one in Kyoto is not as well known.

To deal with the problem of ambiguity, the significance with respect to the target region must be measured. In the same manner as discussed in Section 4.1, we estimated $p(y_i | \text{intitle}(x))$ and $p(y_i | x)$ using values available through search engines. Here, we used "Kyoto" in place of x. The results are shown in Table 3. The results show that most of the highly ranked place names are actually topic terms for Kyoto. This is not surprising if we consider that landmarks are in a sense significant *topics* of the region. Two universities and a shrine did not satisfy the inequality. As a result, Kasuga Shrine, which we considered to be incorrectly ranked, was removed.

Table 3. Place names with frequent appearances of spatial cases.

Place name	SCF	$p(y_i|\text{intitle}(x))$	$p(y_i|x)$
Kyoto Station	19,840	0.1688	0.0327
Kamo River	8,667	0.0450	0.0177
Mount Hiei	6,543	0.0177	0.0085
Kyoto University	6,109	0.2782	0.2742
Yasaka Shrine	4,260	0.0310	0.0076
Kinkakuji Temple	3,919	0.0426	0.0110
Ritsumeikan University	2,886	0.0168	0.0183
Kitano Shrine	2,770	0.0292	0.0056
Heian Shrine	2,723	0.0362	0.0079
Katsura River	2,551	0.0074	0.0047
Ginkakuji Temple	2,276	0.0440	0.0099
Doshisha University	2,149	0.0174	0.0176
Ninnnaji Temple	2,126	0.0172	0.0045
Nanzenji Temple	2,006	0.0276	0.0065
Kasuga Shrine	1,984	0.0002	0.0023

5. Conclusion

We introduced Web aggregate queries. Web aggregate queries are processed through two phases: the probe phase and the validation phase. We described functions to compose various web aggregate queries, and showed that three example queries can be described using these proposed functions.

Acknowledgments

This work was supported in part by a Grant-in-Aid for Scientific Research (No. 18049041) from MEXT of Japan, by a MEXT project entitled "Software Technologies for Search and Integration across Heterogeneous-Media Archives," and by a MEXT 21st Century COE Program entitled "Informatics Research Center for Development of Knowledge Society Infrastructure."

References

1. P. D. Turney, Mining the Web for synonyms: PMI-IR versus LSA on TOEFL, in *ECML*, 2001.
2. S. Oyama and K. Tanaka, Query modification by discovering topics from Web page structures, in *APWEB*, 2004.
3. H. Ohshima, S. Oyama and K. Tanaka, Searching coordinate terms with their context from the Web, in *WISE*, 2006.
4. T. Tezuka, R. Lee, H. Takakura and Y. Kambayashi, Web-based inference rules for processing conceptual geographical relationships, in *W2GIS*, 2001.
5. C. J. Fillmore, *The Case for Case, Universals in Linguistic Theory*, 1968.

PROCESS MINING FOR COMPOSITE WEB SERVICES*

AIQIANG GAO[†] and SHIWEI TANG

*State Key Laboratory of Machine Perception, Peking University,
Beijing, 100871, China*
[†] *E-mail: aqgao@db.pku.edu.cn;tsw@pku.edu.cn*

DONGQING YANG and YAN FU

*School of Electronics Engineering and Computer Science, Peking University,
Beijing, 100871, China*
E-mail: {ydq,fuyan}@db.pku.edu.cn

Web service composition provides a way to build value-added services and web applications by integrating and composing existing web services. A composite web service is essential a process in a loosely-coupled service-oriented architecture. To conduct performance analysis, a workflow representation of the underlying process is required. This paper describes a method to discover such underlying processes from history execution logs. The workflow logs contain temporal information that records the starting and ending time of activities. Based on a probabilistic model, the algorithm can discover sequential, parallel, exclusive choice and iterative structures. Some examples are given to illustrate the algorithm. Though discussed process mining of a composite web service, this method can also be used for mining other workflow applications.

Keywords: Web Service; Composition; Process Mining; workflow.

1. Introduction

The emerging paradigm of web services promises to bring to distributed computation and services the flexibility that the web has brought to the sharing of documents (see Refs. 1). Web service composition[1,2] is to build value-added services and web applications by integrating and composing existing elementary web services(also called component web services).

A composite web service is essential a business process built using SOAs(Service Oriented Architectures) technologies. In some scenarios, to

*This work is supported by the National Natural Science Foundation of China under grant No. 90412010 and 60642004, and the IBM University Joint Research Proposal.

conduct debugging and performance analyzing, a workflow representation is required. Such models are used to evaluate costs, monitor processes, and predict the effect of new policies.[3] For these reasons, empirically building process models from data is of great interest. Such a problem has been called process mining, or simply workflow mining,[10,11] because the usual representation of work processes is workflow graphs.

As far as process mining for a composite web service is concerned, it is to infer the connections between component web services from the log that records the execution of the exported interfaces. This paper gives a method that is based on Markov property[3] to mine the chain of a composite web service from execution logs. The collected logs are assumed to contain temporal information. The whole process is considered to be a sequential one, the nodes of which can be an atomic task, a parallel task, an exclusive task or an iterative task. According to the temporal information and ordering information, the algorithm can identify parallel and exclusive choice constructs. In addition, cycles with arbitrary internal structure but without cycles nesting can be discovered.

This paper is organized as follows: Section 2 describes composite web services and the underlying process model ; Section 3 presents the supporting data structures used in the algorithm; Section 4 discusses an algorithm for mining process model from service execution logs; Section 5 illustrates the algorithms using some examples; Section 6 reviews related works and Section 7 concludes this paper and discusses future work.

2. A Process Model for Composite Web Services

2.1. *Describing Web Services*

For an application to use a web service, the programmatic interface of the web service must be precisely described. WSDL[7] is an XML grammar for specifying properties of a web service such as *what* it does, *where* it is located and *how* it is invoked.

Web service composition is the process of building value-added services and web applications by integrating and composing existing elementary web services. In this paper, the elementary web services that are used to synthesis a composite one are called *component web services*.

BPEL4WS[6] is a specification for composite web service orchestration. The constructs and composition patterns in BPEL4WS can be summarized using workflow patterns discussed by Refs. 4 in detail. The usually used patterns are sequential, conditional choice (exclusive), parallel and iterative.

2.2. *Workflow Graphs*

To make the discussion context of situation, this section begins with introducing the definition of AO graph from Refs. 3.

A workflow graph G is a directed acyclic graph (DAG) where each task is a node, and the parents of a node are its direct pre-requisites. That is, the decision to execute T does not depend on any (other) task in G given its parents. Let an AND/OR workflow graph (AO graph) be a constrained type of DAG, with any node being in one of the following classes:

(1) split node, a node with multiple children;
(2) join node, a node with multiple parents;
(3) simple node, with no more than one parent and no more than one child;

It is required that an AO graph must have exactly one node that has no parents (a *start node*) and exactly one node that has no children (an *end node*). Each task T is an event. It either happens or it does not happen. By an abuse of notation, the same symbols are used to represent both the binary random variables and task events,where $T = 1$ represents the event "T happened". By assuming the Markov condition, a parametric model for a DAG is defined.

2.3. *A Graph-based Model for Composite Web Services*

The workflow graph used in this paper is based on AO-graph discussed in Refs. 3, with cycles allowed. The whole underlying process is considered as a sequential process. Each node of the graph can be simple node, split node or join node. And as far as the sequential chain is concerned, each component can be simple, AND-structure or OR-structure.

The graph is assumed to be "separate", that is, the internal structure of AND or OR can be the same with the whole graph. If any AND or OR structure is separated from the whole graph, it is a workflow graph itself.

Furthermore, a cycle is allowed to be added on a node. Because the internal structure of cycle can be any combination of simple, AND and OR, cycles are not allowed to nest with each other. A case where this assumption makes sense is illustrated by Fig. 1. In this example, by the assumption of no cycles nesting, the algorithm can determine that the cycle case is "A" without considering another nesting cycle as "B".

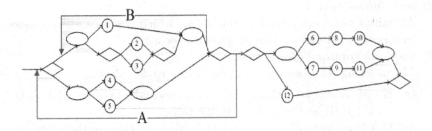

Fig. 1. cycles at different position. When the log contains sequence as $1, 2, 1, 3, \cdots$ and $1, 2, 4, 5, \cdots$, it is not sure whether cycle A or both A and B is the correct structure.

3. Supporting Data Structures

3.1. *Execution Logs*

Suppose the execution log $L = \{L_1, L_2, \cdots, L_m\}$ consists of m records each describing a execution trace of a business instance.

Each record is a sequence of log elements: *service(starttime, endtime)*, separated by comma. Each log element represents an execution of *service* starting at time *starttime* and ending at time *endtime*.

For a parallel construct(AND-split and AND-join), the logs are complete, i.e. the combination of any two parallel branches are present in log.

For a mutually exclusive choice construct, the logs are complete. All children of an *OR-split* are contained in the log file. This guarantees that the whole exclusive choice can be derived.

For an iterative construct, the logs are complete. If there are two mutually exclusive branches in the internal of a cycle, this condition helps determine the position of the cycle, which is illustrated in Fig. 1.

A log record is documented according to the temporal order of the tasks. If A starts executing earlier than B, A is before B in the log.

3.2. *Supporting Data Structure*

The procedure for process mining may scan the log file many times. To reduce the number of I/Os substantially, the log is preprocessed and stored in a relational database.

(1) *tasks(taskid, sojourntime)*
   All the tasks occurring in the log are stored in relation *tasks*.

(2) *task_initial(taskid)*

All initial tasks are stored in this table, which contains all the tasks that occur at the first place of some log record.

(3) *task_ordering(taskid, nexttaskid)*

The ordering relationship are inserted into *task_ordering*.

    (a) If task A and task B are observable descendants of an AND-split, both (A, B) and (B, A) are in the table.

    (b) If A is an immediate ancestor of B, then (A,B) is in the table.

    (c) For exclusive tasks A and B, neither (A,B) nor (B,A) is allowed.

(4) *task_cross(taskid, crosstaskid, label, timestamp)*

For two tasks A and B in a log line, if one of the following happens, task A and B are called *crossing tasks*. (a)$start_A \leq start_B \leq end_A$; (b) $start_A \leq end_B \leq end_A$.

This table stores the temporal crossing, where *label* can be "start" or "end" depending on which crossing case happens.

(5) *task_freq(loginx, taskid, frequency)*

At last, to identify a loop in the process, the occurrence frequencies of each task in a log line are recorded in this table.

This paper also defines the following operations.

(1) $Crossing(a) = \{b|b \in tasks \wedge (a, b) \in tasks\_cross\}$

(2) $EquivalentCross(set) = \{a|\forall b \in set, Crossing(a) = Crossing(b)\}$

(3) *CrossClosure* is defined on a task set using *Crossing* operation.

It defines a set of tasks that is the closure of the input according to *Crossing*. At each iteration, $Crossing(a)$ is computed for each task $a \in set$. And the union of *set* and all $Crossing(a)$ are computed. If no changes occur, the iteration terminates; else, the procedure continues.

(4) $EquivalentOrdering(set) = \{a|\forall b \in set, (a, b) \in task\_ordering \vee (b, a) \in task\_ordering\}$

4. Process Mining Method

4.1. *Main Algorithm*

Algorithm 1 outlines the main steps for mining a process. Here, only a higher-level description is present. Other sub-algorithms that are referred to by the main algorithm are given in Subsection 4.2.

Algorithm 1 builds the whole sequential chain by iteratively adding nodes to it. Different from Refs. 3, where at each step all the task nodes that do not have any children in current graph are added to the graph, this algorithm generates a subgraph for all such tasks and their cross closure. This algorithm deals with a whole "AND" or "OR" subgraph at a time, where Refs. 3 deals with only the "leaves" of the current workflow graph.

Algorithm 1 Processing Mining
1: get all tasks and initial tasks into *alltasks* and *initialtasks*,respectively;
2: *cross* ← *getCrossClosure(initialtasks)*;
3: *currGraph* ← *getGraph_loop(cross, false)*;
4: *alltasks.removeAll(cross)*;
5: **while** !*alltasks.isEmpty()* **do**
6:     *nexttasks* ← *getNextTasks(cross)*;
7:     *cross* ← *getCrossClosure(nexttasks)*;
8:     *nextgraph* ← *getGraph_loop(cross, false)*;
9:     *currgraph* ← *connectgraph(currgraph, nextgraph)*;
10:    *alltasks.removeAll(cross)*;
11: **end while**

4.2. Sub-Algorithms Details

Algorithm 2 generates a subgraph for input tasks set **incross**. Firstly, it calls *checkCycle* to check whether **incross** is contained by a loop. If there is a loop, a subgraph object with *type* = *"loop"* is generated and this procedure is called recursively with a flag indicating that a cycle has been found. Because the cycles are assumed not to nest with each other, the remaining steps don't consider cycles any more.

Algorithm 2 Get a SubGraph
1: **if** cycles not found yet **then**
2:    *checkCycle(incross)*;
3:    new a subgraph with type "loop" and call *getGraph_loop(incross, true)*;
4: **end if**
5: **if** *incross.size()* == 1 **then**
6:    new a *SubGraph* object with type "atomic" and return;
7: **end if**
8: take an element *a* from *incross* and compute its closure *crossa*;
9: **if** *crossa.equals(incross)* **then**
10:    divide *crossa* into subsets whose elements have the same value under cross relation;
11:    new a *SubGraph* object with type "And";
12:    call *getGraph_loop* for each subset, and the result to "And" object;
13: **else**
14:   **if** *incross* ⊃ *crossa* **then**
15:     divide *incross* into subsets according to cross;

16:    new an "OR" subgraph object;
17:    insert resulting graph for each subset into "OR" object;
18: **else**
19:    divide *incross* into subsets according to ordering relation;
20:    new a "chain" object if the number of subsets is 1;
21:    new an "OR" subgraph object and insert the subgraph for each subset;
22: **end if**
23:**end if**

The procedure of checking cycles is described in Algorithm 3. It works in the following way.

Algorithm 3 Check Cycles
1: take $a \in incross$ and compute its closure *crossa*;
2: **if** $crossa.equals(incross)$ **then**
3:    divide *crossa* into subsets according to *EquivalentCross*;
4:    **for** $subset \leftarrow$ one of the subsets **do**
5:        $logids \leftarrow$ all log ids where *subset* occurs more than once;
6:        **if** $tset \in subsets \setminus subset$ occur more than once in $logid \in logids$ **then**
7:            **find a loop**;
8:        **else if** *tset* is an "OR" node **then**
9:            **find a loop** if more than two "OR" branches occurs;
10:       **end if**
11:       **if** no subset occurs more than once **then**
12:           **find a loop** if more than two "OR" branches occurs;
13:       **end if**
14:   **end for**
15: **end if**
16: **if** not $crossa.equals(incross)$ **then**
17:    compute all "OR" branches of **incross**;
18:    **find a loop** if more than two "OR" branches occurs in a same log;
19: **end if**

If the current node being checked is an "AND" one, it checks if there is some branches occurring more than once in a single log record. If the answer is **yes**, check the other branches to make sure a cycle. If all the other branches are checked to occur only once, the cycle is not covering the current node but one of its branches. If the answer is **no**(i.e. there is no branches occurring more than once) and more than two "OR" branches occurs in a same log record, the "AND" node is also to be in a cycle.

If the current node being checked is an "OR" one, it checks if more than one branch occurs in a same log record. If the result is yes, a loop is found.

5. Illustration Examples

To illustrate the execution of algorithms in Section 4, some examples are described here. This section begins with the example in Refs. 3. Then cycles are added to different position of this example. Furthermore, some single-task branches are changed into a task chain to illustrate that the combination of crossing and ordering do the job.

Figure 2 corresponds to the original model. All the tasks in this graph are recorded in the log. In this example, the initial tasks is $\{1, 2, 3, 4, 5\}$ and its cross closure is $\{1, 2, 3, 4, 5\}$.

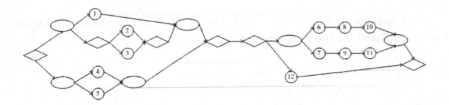

Fig. 2.   An example workflow graph

According to algorithm 2, the cross closure of any element in $\{1, 2, 3, 4, 5\}$ is not equal to itself, so the structure is of "OR" type. Then it is divided into two subset, with $\{1, 2, 3, 4, 5\} = \{1, 2, 3\} \cup \{4, 5\}$.

When $\{1, 2, 3\}$ is fed to *getGraph_loop*, it is found that the cross closure of element 1 is equal to $\{1, 2, 3\}$. So, the subgraph for $\{1, 2, 3\}$ is of type "AND". Then, $\{4, 5\}$ is input to *getGraph_loop*. It is found that $crossclosure(4) = crossclosure(5) = \{4, 5\}$, so this is an "AND" structure.

After two "OR" branches, a "OR" structure is generated. Then, the algorithm removes $\{1, 2, 3, 4, 5\}$ from **alltasks** and begins the iteration.

The next tasks for $\{1, 2, 3, 4, 5\}$ is $\{6, 7, 12\}$ by *getNextTasks*, whose cross closure is $\{6, 7, 8, 9, 10, 11, 12\}$. After *getGraph_loop* is executed, this set corresponds to an "OR" structure, with two branches for $\{6, 7, 8, 9, 10, 11\}$ and $\{12\}$, respectively.

After the "OR" structure for $\{6, 7, 8, 9, 10, 11, 12\}$ is generated, it is connected to the subgraph for $\{1, 2, 3, 4, 5\}$. The resulting graph is exactly the original graph as Fig. 2.

Now, some extra data is added for a cycle. Suppose a log record with two occurrence of task 1, and one occurrence for task 2 and 3. When *get-Graph_loop* is called for $\{1, 2, 3\}$, the *checkCycle* procedure will execute lines 5-7. The result is that a cycle is found, whose internal structure is the result of calling *getGraph_loop* for $\{1, 2, 3\}$. Figure 3 illustrates this situation.

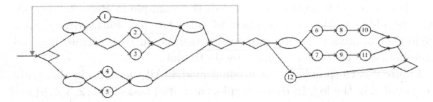

Fig. 3.   An example workflow graph with cycle

Let's assume that the atomic task 2 is replaced with a chain containing two tasks 2 and 2', the graph is Fig. 4.

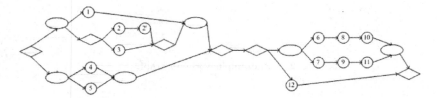

Fig. 4.   Another example of workflow graph

6. Related Works

Agrawal et al.[9] introduced the first algorithm for mining workflow logs. Greco et al.[11] approach the problem using clustering techniques. A broad survey on the current work in workflow mining, or process mining,is given by van der Aalst and Wejters in Refs. 10.

The problem of automatic process discovery is based on a probability model,[3,8] i.e. by assuming Markov condition. The method discussed in this paper for deriving process model is mostly motivated by Refs. 3. The basic model used here is adopted from that work with non-nesting cycles allowed. The differences are: In this paper, the log is read and loaded into database for further use. The ordering and crossing relation are all computed from the log with temporal information. With the frequency of task in a single log record, this paper can also discover non-nesting cycles.

Challenges on process mining are proposed in Refs. 10 such as hidden tasks, duplicate tasks, non-free-choice constructs, loops, noise and lack of completeness. Those problems will be further discussed in future work.

7. Conclusion

This paper discusses an algorithm for mining workflow graph for a composite web service. It works on base of the temporal information in the log. By reasoning about the crossing closure of a task set, the algorithm can deduce whether a complex structure is an "AND" or "OR". Examples have been analyzed to illustrate the algorithm. More extensive experiments are needed for this work. Noise in log data will also be explored in future work.

References

1. R. Hull, M. Benedikt, V. Christophides, and J. Su, E-services: A look behind the curtain. In Proc. ACM Symp. on Principles of Database Systems, 2003.
2. Aphrodite Tsalgatidou, Thomi Pilioura, An Overview of Standards and Related Technology in Web Services, Distributed and Parallel Databases, 12, 125–162, 2002.
3. Ricardo Silva, Jiji Zhang, James G. Shanahan, Probabilistic Workflow Mining, KDD'05, August 21–24, 2005, Chicago, Illinois, USA.
4. W. M. P. van der Aalst, A. H. M. ter Hofstede, B. Kiepuszewski, and A. P. Barros, Workflow Patterns. Distributed and Parallel Databases, 14(1): 5–51, 2003.
5. V. G. Kulkarni, Operations Research Applied Stochastic Models (photocopy), Beijing: Tsinghua Press, China, 2004.
6. Business Process Execution Language for Web Services, version 1.1, http://www.ibm.com/developerworks/library/ws-bpel/.
7. W3C, "Web Services Description Language (WSDL) Version 2.0", W3C Working Draft, March 2003. (See http://www.w3.org/TR/wsdl20/.)
8. J. Klingemann, J. Wsach, and K. Aberer, Deriving Service Models in Cross-Organizational Workflows. In Ninth International Workshop on Research Issues in Data Engineering: Virtual Enterprise, RIDE-VE'99, Sydney, Australia, March 1999.
9. R. Agrawal, D. Gunopulos, and F. Leymann, Mining process models from work-flow logs. Proc. of 6th International Conference on Extending Database Technology, pages 469–483, 1998.
10. Aalst and A. J. M. M. Weijters, Process Mining: A Research Agenda. Computers in Industry, 53(3): 231–244, 2004.
11. G. Greco, A. Guzzo, L. Pontieri, and D. Sacca, Mining expressive process models by clustering workflow traces. Proc. of the 8th PAKDD, 2004.

WEB RESOURCE CATEGORIZATION FOR SEMANTIC WEB SEARCH

MINGHUA PEI, KOTARO NAKAYAMA, TAKAHIRO HARA and SHOJIRO NISHIO

Graduate School of Information Science and Technology,
Osaka University, Japan
E-mail: {hai.meika, nakayama.kotaro, hara, nishio}@ist.osaka-u.ac.jp

In Semantic Web search, the resource type that does not exist in the ontology becomes to be a big issue. In this paper, we propose a Web resource categorization method for Semantic Web Search to search the classes that have high relation to the user's intent. Our proposed categorization method infers relations between classes even without explicit definitions, by using the construction of classes in ontologies and the associations between classes and properties in RDFs. Finally, we confirm the effectivity of the proposed approach by comparing with conventional approaches.

1. Introduction

Recently, the Semantic Web is showing an increase in size and variety of resources because the large spate of unstructured, heterogeneous resources on the Internet make it difficult for users to find the information they really need. A new concept, the Semantic Web, appends semantic information, which is machine readable and understandable, to Web resources, thus making the use of Web resources more efficient. Many works have been presented for generating Semantic Web resources,[4] ranking Semantic Web documents,[3] and processing approximate query for Semantic Web search such as Corese.[1] However, these conventional methods are proposed based on well-structured ontologies. As the WWW changes dynamically, and relations are missed in the collecting process, these methods cannot match the resource types having no relation in the ontology. Therefore, to detect the potential relations with existing ontologies becomes an important and emerging issue to efficiently use Web resources.

For this purpose, we propose a categorization method which infers relations between classes even without explicit definitions. We attempt to detect the related and the potentially related Web resources by analyzing the existing ontologies and dictionaries. We focus on some factors from the concept structure, the syntax in dictionary and the relation existed in Web resources. We defined an algorithm based on each of the factor to perform the categorization. By using our proposed method, the Web resources related to the categories can be categorized by using both the explicit definitions and the detected relations. As the result, it would provide more possibility to semantically match the user queries.

We also evaluate our proposed method by implementing it on a Semantic Web search engine and adopting it to search Web resources. The results show that our method can significantly increase the efficiency of information retrieval.

The rest of the paper is organized as follows: Section 2 describes our proposed categorization method. Section 3 presents an experiment for evaluating our proposed method. Finally, we conclude the paper in Sec. 4.

2. Categorization Algorithm

2.1. *Approach*

As problems such as a lack of relations and missing definitions always exist in real world Semantic Web data, the central idea of our approach is to categorize the resource types by using not only well-defined relations but also some possible semantic relations for incompleted ontologies. We take into account four factors as follows.

The first factor is the relations of classes defined in Web ontologies. According to the definition, all extended classes based on the properties such as "rdf:subClassOf," "owl:equivalentClass" and "owl:sameAs" should be in the same category. The second is the relations between class name and category. Sometimes, a class can be identified from another class which has the same class name in different namespaces. For example, the class with the name "student" always belongs to "Person." If we get these word relations, we can extend the category by the classes whose names are in those words. The third is the word relations defined in ordinary dictionaries (we used WordNet). Because there are some classes having little information to categorize them, we can categorize them by using the general meaning of the class name and the relations of the words in dictionaries. The last factor is the relations between the property patterns and category. In RDFs, a number of properties are used to describe a Web resource. The association between properties and category will be helpful for providing a deeper categorization.

Algorithm $Process\ 1(A)$
1: **Foreach** $(category\ a \in A)$
2:   **Foreach** $(class\ c_0 \in a)$
3:     $RER(c_0, a, r_{c_0,a})$;
Function $RER(c_0, a, r_{c_0,a})$
1: **Foreach** $(class\ c \in c_0.Children)$
2:   $r_{c,a} = 0.95 \times r_{c_0,a}$;
3:   **If** $(c.Contain(a) = false)$
4:     $a.Add(c, r_{c,a})$;
5:     $RER(c, a, r_{c,a})$;
6: **Foreach** $(class\ c \in c.Equivalents)$
7:   $r_{c,a} = r_{c_0,a}$;
8:   **If** $(c.Contain(a) = false)$
9:     $a.Add(c, r_{c,a})$;
10:     $RER(c, a, r_{c,a})$;

Algorithm $Process\ 2(A, minW)$
1: **Foreach** $(category\ a \in A)$
2:   **Foreach** $(classname$
        $cName \in getName(a))$
3:     $l = getW(cName, a)$;
4:     **If** $(l > minW)$
5:     **Foreach** $(class$
        $c \in getClass(cName))$
6:       **If** $(c.Contain(a) = false)$
7:       $r_{c,a} = avg(getR(cName, a)) \times k$;
8:       $a.Add(c, r_{c,a})$;
9:   $Process1(A)$
Function $getW(i, j)$
1: $W_{i,j} = tf_{i,j} \times log\frac{N}{df_i}$;
2: $W'_{i,j} = \frac{W_{i,j}}{max(W_{i,j})}$;
3: **Return** $W'_{i,j}$;

Algorithm $Process\ 3(A, minW)$
1: **Foreach** $(category\ a \in A)$
2:   **Foreach** $(classname$
        $cName \in getName(a))$
3:     $B = cName.Children$;
4:     **Foreach** $(classname\ wd \in B)$
5:       **Foreach** $(class\ c \in getClass(wd))$
6:         **If** $(c.Contain(a) = false)$
7:         $r_{c,a} = avg(getR(wd_0, a)) \times 0.95$;
8:         $a.Add(c, r_{c,a})$;
9:   $Process\ 2(A, minW)$

Algorithm $Process\ 4(A, minf, minW)$
1: **Foreach** $(category\ a \in A)$
2:   $P_a = getPattern(a)$;
3:   **Foreach** $(propertyset\ p \in P_a)$
4:     $x = f(p)$;
5:     **If** $(length(p) = 1)$
6:     **If** $(x > minf)$
7:       $P_a.Delete(p)$;
8:     **Else**
9:     **If** $(x > minf)$
10:       **Foreach** $(class\ c \in getType(p))$
11:         **If** $(c.Contain(a) = false)$
12:         $r_{c,a} = avg(getR_p(p, a))$
          $\times \frac{\frac{N}{N}+1}{2}$;
13:         $a.Add(c, r_{c,a})$;
14:     $P_a.Delete(p)$;
15:   $Process\ 2(A, minW)$

Fig. 1. Algorithm of 4 processes.

We define four processes based on each of the factors mentioned above, as shown in Fig. 1, to perform the categorization.

Before executing the four processes, we defined several typical categories that are frequently used in searching queries, such as "Person", "Animal", "Event", and "Location." A denotes a set of these categories specified for categorization, and a denotes a category in A. This denotation is used in each process. We defined some class names to get base classes for each category, and the relation strength of initial classes to the category equals 1.

2.2. Process 1: Categorize Offspring

In *Process* 1, we categorize the classes based on a hierarchical structure of classes. If a class has a relation to a category, its subclasses ("rdf:subClassOf") also have a relation, which is a little bit weaker than that of their super classes, to the category. The equivalent classes ("owl:equivalentClass" and "owl:sameAs") have equivalent relation strength.

Process 1 is performed by using a recursive function $RER(c_0, a, r_{c_0,a})$. Let c_0 be a class in a category a with the relation strength as $r_{c_0,a}$. $RER(c_0, a, r_{c_0,a})$ can categorize the class c, which is an equivalent class or a subclass of the class c_0 to category a with relation strength as $r_{c,a}$. By recursively calling itself, $RER(c_0, a, r_{c_0,a})$ categorizes all the offspring classes of c_0. Here, we give a coefficient k for the degressive strength of relation in the hierarchical structure. We specify k as 1 for a same level and as 0.95 for a lower level based on some preliminary experiments. The relation strength of class c to category a, $r_{c,a}$, can be calculated by following Eq. (1).

$$r_{c,a} = k \times r_{c_0,a}, \tag{1}$$

$$k = \begin{cases} 1 & \text{"owl:equivalentClass"} \\ & \text{or " owl: sameAs,"} \\ 0.95 & \text{"rdf:subClassOf."} \end{cases} \tag{2}$$

2.3. *Process 2: Extend Category Based on Characteristic Class Name*

Based on the results of *Process* 1, we have categorized some classes for each category. Then we take notice of the class names that represent the characters of a category. We consider that the classes having the characteristic class names of category a can also be categorized into a.

In *Process* 2, we categorize the classes based on the important class names. This category extension consists of two steps, extraction of important class names for each category and categorization of the classes having these class names as well as the offspring classes of the newly categorized classes. The algorithm is described in the concrete as follows.

For each category a, we extract all the class names by function $getName(a)$. Then we compute a coefficient l to evaluate how much a class name $cName$ can represent the character of a by function $getW(cName, a)$ which is based on tfidf.[5] Since tfidf in text retrieval can extract the words that are particularly important to a document, we attempt to find out the important class names of each category by using tfidf. The weight of class name i in category j is denoted by $W_{i,j}$, which is calculated by Eq. (3).

$$W_{i,j} = tf_{i,j} \times log(\frac{N}{df_i}), \tag{3}$$

$$tf_{i,j} = \text{number of occurrences of } i \text{ in } j,$$
$$df_i = \text{number of categories containing } i,$$
$$N = \text{total number of categories in } A.$$

Since $W_{i,j}$ is largely affected by the number of classes in a category, we normalize $W_{i,j}$ in $[0,1]$, and $W'_{i,j}$ denotes the normalized value which can be calculated by Eq. (4).

$$W'_{i,j} = \frac{W_{i,j}}{max(W_{i,j})}. \tag{4}$$

We give a threshold $minW$ for $W'_{i,j}$, specified as 0.02 in our experiment by considering both the effectivity and the cost of categorization. We consider the class names having $W'_{i,j}$ larger than $minW$ as the important class names for the category. For each important class name $cName$, we extract all the classes having class name $cName$ of category a from all the classes by function $getClass(cName)$. From these classes, we extend category a with each class c which denotes a class having a class name as $cName$ but not existing in category a. For a set of classes having class name $cName$ and existing in category a, $getR(cName, a)$ is a function to get the relation strengths of the classes in the set to category a, and $avg(getR(cName, a))$ denotes the average. Then, the relation strength of class c to the category a can be calculated by Eq. (5).

$$r_{c,a} = avg(getR(cName, a)) \times W'_{i,j}. \tag{5}$$

As the second step, we extend the categories with all the offspring classes of the newly categorized classes by executing $Process$ 1 again.

2.4. *Process 3: Detect Potential Relation from Dictionary*

Process 3 extends the categories based on the superior-inferior relation between words in WordNet. There is an "is-a" relationship between superior and inferior words in the dictionary. However, there also exist many multisense words that are not in common use. Thus, we take into account the single-sense words that we can get from the words having only one superior in the dictionary. The algorithm is described in the concrete as follows.

We get all the class names in category a by function $getName(a)$. Then, we prune the class names that exist in more than one category. For each class name $cName \in getName(a)$, we extract all the offspring class names from WordNet and store them in B. For each class name wd in B, we get all the classes whose class name is wd. If these classes do not exist in category a, they are categorized into a.

Since an "is-a" relationship can be considered as an extension to a lower level, we compute relation strength based on that of classes having a superior class name. $r_{c,a}$ denotes the relation strength of class c having class name wd to category a. wd_0 denotes the superior of wd, and $getR(wd_0, a)$ computes the relation strength between classes having class name as the superior of wd to category a. $avg(getR(wd_0, a))$ denotes their average. Then, $r_{c,a}$ can be calculated by Eq. (6).

$$r_{c,a} = avg(getR(wd_0, a)) \times 0.95. \tag{6}$$

Then, we execute *Process* 2 again to extend categories with all the offspring classes having root names with high tfidf values.

2.5. *Process 4: Detect Relation by Property Pattern Analysis*

In *Process* 4, we have a deeper categorization based on property patterns. In the Semantic Web, one resource is usually described by several properties. Here, we define a property set as a set of properties that describe the same resource. Then, a property pattern is defined as a property set that satisfies the following two assumptions. First, a property pattern describes the Web resources that exist in only one category. Second, the number of Web resources described by a property pattern should be no less than a threshold *minf*. The number of properties in a property pattern is defined as length of the pattern.

The pattern discovery is implemented based on the co-occurrence of properties in describing the Web resources that are categorized based on the categorized classes. Therefore, the result of pattern discovery is closely related to the previous categorization. Let p_k denote a property pattern whose length is k, p_{k+1} denote a property pattern whose length is $k + 1$, and $p_k \subset p_{k+1}$. Then, Web resources described by p_{k+1} contain the Web resources described by p_k. Therefore, we extract property patterns from short ones to long ones, and when we generate a longer property set candidate, we don't need to consider the property sets containing short property patterns, and we don't extract patterns having length of 1 for its high casualness. In another effort to get reliable extension, we extract the patterns that appeared more than $minf$. The threshold $minf$ can be specified by IR system developers based on some preliminary experiments. In our experiment, the categorization shows almost same results when $minf \geq 4$, hence we specify *minf*=4 here.

By using property patterns, we can categorize the Web resources that cannot be categorized based on the three previous processes.

Then we extend categories by using the extended resource types and all their offspring classes. For example, we realized that a property set "http://xmlns.com/foaf/0.1/name" and "http://xmlns.com/foaf/0.1/weblog" frequently co-occur in category "Person" but don't co-occur in other categories. This means that the property pattern describes the Web resources that belong to category "Person". Then we categorize all the resource types described by this property pattern as "Person". At the same time, we detected some resource types such as "http://xmlns.com/foaf/0.1/maker" using the property pattern in *Process* 4. "http://xmlns. com/foaf/0.1/maker" was not categorized in *Processes* 1 and 2 because of no relation data existing in the ontology of this experiment. It was also not detected in *Process* 3 because of the multisense in the dictionary.

Process 4 can be described as follows. We compute the entire property set, denoted by P_a, of category a by function $getPatten(a)$. For each property set p in P_a, function $f(p)$ counts x, the number of the resources described by p. When the length of p is 1, the property set p having x larger than $minf$ is deleted from P_a. When the length of p is larger than 1 and its x is larger than $minf$, we extract all the resource types, which are classes, related to p by using function $getType(p)$. Then, we extend category a with class c which is extracted by $getType(p)$ and does not exist in a.

We calculate the relations by considering the frequency of the property pattern in categorized RDFs. In a category a, N is the count of the resources in a, and N_r is the count of resources described by property pattern p. We can get the relation strengths of classes related to property pattern p to category a by using function $getR_p(p, a)$. $avg(getR_p(p, a))$ denotes their average. Then, the relation strength of the detected class c to category a can be calculated by following equation (7).

$$r_{c,a} = avg(getR_p(p, a)) \times \frac{(\frac{N_r}{N} + 1)}{2}. \tag{7}$$

Since some classes are newly categorized from the resource type, we execute *Process* 2 again to extend the category using those newly categorized classes.

2.6. *Flow of Whole Categorization*

The whole flow of the proposed categorization method is performed in the order of algorithms from *Process* 1 to 4. As shown in Fig. 1, previous processes become a part of next process in *Processes* 2 to 4.

As described above, *Processes* 1, 2 and 3 are used to categorize more classes and *Process* 4 is directly concerned with Web resources. Thus, when the classes are categorized, *Process* 2 and *Process* 3 are more efficient. When the Web resources are categorized well, *Process* 4 should be the most efficient factor for the IR system.

3. Experiment for CSWS

In this experiment, we developed a Categorization-based Semantic Web Search (CSWS) system to examine the proposed method.

There are two important measurements used to compare the accuracy of information retrieval, *precision* and *recall*. For a given user and a given query, assume that the user marked all the Web resources being relevant or irrelevant to the query. Let A denote a set of the relevant resources marked by the users, B denote a set of the IR results that are the resources output by CSWS, and C denote the intersection of A and B, i.e., the common resources of the IR results and the relevant resources. Then, *precision* is the ratio of the common resources to the relevant resources, and *recall* is the ratio of the common resources to the IR results.

$$Precision = \frac{|C|}{|B|},\eqno(8)$$

$$Recall = \frac{|C|}{|A|}.\eqno(9)$$

An important fact is that increasing *precision* will often cause decreasing *recall*. In our approach (CSWS), the goal of the search is to answer user's in-explicit queries with the results having high relations that are either defined in the ontologies or discovered in an analysis process. Therefore, increasing *recall* should come before that of *precision*.

3.1. *Data Sources and Evaluations*

We performed an experiment of categorization and adopted the results to an SWS engine to evaluate the proposed method with the two measures, *precision* and *recall*. In this experiment, we used Google API to find URLs of documents that are likely to be Semantic Web data sources. Since Semantic Web data sources typically use special file extensions such as rdf, owl and xml, the crawler gathers files with such extensions. About 150,000 triples are extracted for relations of classes. We collected over 111,000 classes, among which there are about 9% classed as not existing in the ontology. In the

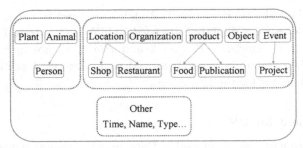

Fig. 2. Categories

experiment data, there are about 8,000 resources, which have 535 resource types, used in the experiment, and 45% resources, 66% resource types that do not exist in the ontology. We defined the categories statistically based on the classes. After counting the appearances, we defined several categories as shown in Fig. 2, where some categories are defined as sub-categories. A class, which can be categorized to a sub-category, would not be categorized into its super-category to remove the effect of correlation among categories.

By using such data sources, we implemented our proposed categorization method and got the categories of classes and categories of Web resources. In our experiment, about 19.2% classes are categorized based on the class categorization, and about 38.2% of Web resources are categorized. The rate of categorized classes is low in this experiment due to the following two reasons. First, a lack of relations seriously exists in our experiment ontology, and we only used a small amount of Web resources. Second, we have not optimized the parameters because of considering the cost of performance. Thus, it may lead to a higher resource categorization to complement the ontology and optimize the parameters.

In this research, we mainly focus on Web resource categorization for Semantic Web search. In the experiment, we have chosen Target 1 and Target 2 for baselines because both of them are based on very popular approaches for Semantic Web search. Target 1 is based on class specification like Swoogle,[2] one of the most popular Semantic Web search engines. Target 2 is based on concept similarity that is another popular approach. In Target 2, users can specify the search target as a class tree, which contains all the offspring classes of the root. Then the system searches all the resources whose types are in the class tree. Many IR methods such as Corese are based on this approach. CSWS retrieves the Web resources from the category that is specified by the users and provides the results containing the keyword. On the other hand, we consider that Web resources described by more

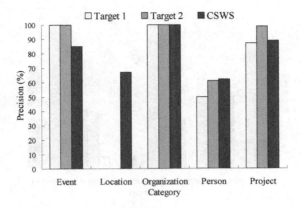

Fig. 3.   Comparison for precision.

properties can provide more information to users. Thus, we rank the result by the count of properties describing the Web resources.

To evaluate the search results with *precision* and *recall*, we made a set of relevant recourses based on some questionnaire data. We randomly chose 5 keywords such as knowledge, social, etc. as queries. Each keyword returns 30 to 60 results from the whole resources. Then we let 10 users (university students) manually categorize the results into the categories we specified in Fig. 2. We used the whole answers marked by the users as *relevant* resources. For example, if a resource x is marked as category a_1 and a_2, then the resource x is not only used as a relevant resource of category a_1 but also used as a relevant resource of category a_2. By using the same 5 keywords, we get the results from our proposed CSWS (or Target 1, Target 2) as IR results (B) and the intersection of A and $B(C)$ to calculate *precision* and *recall*.

3.2. *Evaluation Results*

In the result, we got *precision* and *recall* for 5 categories: "Event", "Location", "Organization", "Person" and "Project." According to the results in Fig. 3 and Fig. 4, extending the classes for the category is effective to provide search results with better accuracy.

In Fig. 3, CSWS can provide search results having *precision* as high as Target 1 and Target 2. As a result of category extension, CSWS can find the related results without explicit definition for the relation to the user query. In the second category, the search engine didn't find any result for "Location" in Target 1 and Target 2 because there is no resource defined as

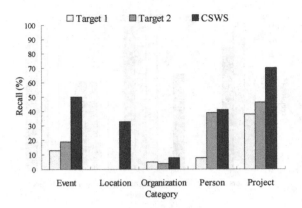

Fig. 4. Comparison for recall.

location or subclasses of location in our ontologies. However, CSWS could find some items, such as bus station, as the results for location based on our proposed categorization method. Therefore, while an extended category probably has a lower *precision* in some categories, it can also provide some highly related results without the user's explicit specification. As shown in Fig. 4, CSWS has the highest *recall* in most categories.

3.3. *Comparison with Corese*

As a similarity-based Semantic Web search engine, Corese can provide an advanced query processing. Corese can search both the directly related and indirectly related Web resources. For example, assume that a user wants to retrieve the organizations related to "human science." There is a member of an organization, and the member is interested in "human science." Then this organization can be considered as an organization related to "human science." Corese also contributed to improving *recall* by using direct relation and proximate relation. Thus, for a well-structured ontology, Corese can present high precision and recall.

Currently, CSWS cannot find this kind of relation, because it provides a category matching method. However, our proposed method can categorize some Web resources whose types do not exist in the ontology by detecting the probably-related resource types. When a user wants to retrieve organizations related to "human science," CSWS could look into not only the Web resources defined as an organization but also some Web resources be inferred as a kind of organization. For example, in our experiment data, for a resource type "ns:WorkingGroup", we only know it has a parent class as "ns:Group." There is no relation between this resources type and organization in other ontologies. For this kind of case, this resource type would not be considered relating to organization by Corese. However, by considering the relations between class names and categories, this resource type might be considered a kind of organization by CSWS.

In real world Semantic Web, it is impossible to construct a completed ontology. It is clear that the ontology would become a limitation for the methods based on well-structured ontologies. On the contrary, CSWS might provide high recall in real world data by detecting the relations.

4. Conclusions

In this paper, we proposed a categorization method for Semantic Web resources by integrating the categorization and SWS techniques. We confirmed that CSWS can provide users better search results having high relations to the users' needs without explicit queries by extending the categories. Since the real world Semantic Web dynamically changes, it is impossible to construct a perfect ontology by any one organization. Therefore, to make an integrative use for the published ontology becomes more important. We believe that our approach is an attempt for practical use of Semantic Web resources.

As part of our future work, we plan to study in more detail which factor is effective for the total accuracy. An optimal coordination for an integrative categorization can improve the method of categorization and apply to a large Web resource database. To improve the accuracy of the categorization, we need to optimize the parameters.

References

1. O. Corby, R. Dieng-Kuntz, and C Faron-Zucker, "Querying the Semantic Web with the Corese Search Engine," Proc. of ECAI/PAIS, 2004.
2. L. Ding, T. Finin, A. Joshi, R. Pan, R. S. Cost, Y. Peng, P. Reddivari, V. C. Doshi, and J. Sachs, "Swoogle: A Search and Metadata Engine for the Semantic Web," Proc. of ACM Conf. on Information and Knowledge Management, 2004.
3. R. Guha, R. McCool, and E. Miller, "Semantic Search," Proc. of the International Conf. on World Wide Web, pp. 700–709, 2003.
4. N. F. Noy, M. Sintek, S. Decker, M. Crubezy, R. W. Fergerson, and M. A. Musen, "Creating Semantic Web Contents with Protege-2000," IEEE Intelligent Systems, Vol. 16, Issue 2, pp. 60–71, 1997.
5. G. Salton, M. McGill, "Introduction to Modern Information Retrieval," McGraw-Hill Book Company, 1984.

AN EFFECTIVE TOP-K DATA SOURCES RANKING
APPROACH ON DEEP WEB*

LI MEIFANG, WANG GUANGQI, SHEN DERONG, NIE TIEZHENG, ZHU HONGKAI
and YU GE

Dept. of Computer Sci. and Eng., Northeastern University, Shenyang, 110004, China

Query on deep web has been gaining great importance due to the large amount of deep web data sources. Inspired by the observations on deep web, the paper presents a novel top-k ranking strategy to rank the relevant data sources according to the user's requirement. First, it applies an attribute based frequent pattern growth algorithm to mining the most dominant attributes, and then employs a dominance and relevance based top-k style ranking algorithm to find the relevant data sources with early candidates pruning and termination, which has proved high efficiency. We have conducted extensive experiments on a real world dataset and demonstrated the efficiency of our approach.

1. Introduction

At present, the rapid growth and prevalence of data sources on deep web have been drawing great attentions all over the world [1, 2]. A significant amount of information is now hidden on the deep web, since data can "only" be dynamically accessed through query interfaces. Survey in April 2004 estimated 450,000 online databases, with 307,000 deep web sources and over 1.2 million query interfaces [1], and richer with web developing. On deep web, information cannot be accessed directly through static URL links but only available as responses to dynamic queries submitted through the query interface. Thereby, though there are myriad useful data sources online, users are often still confronted with the problem of finding the right sources. Besides, how to select the most useful data resources is also a challenging issue. Therefore, the theme of this paper focuses on finding the most relevant data sources, thus ranking and retrieving the top-k sources to the user, especially under the study of deep web.

Survey [1] indicates two important features of deep web: 1) proliferating sources: as the web scales, many existing data sources tend to provide structured information in the same domains; 2) converging vocabularies: the aggregate schema of sources in the same domain tends to converge at small size. Studies

* This work is supported by the National Science Foundation (60673139, 60573090), the National High-Tech Development Program (2003AA414210).

have observed sources under deep web conform to Zipf-like distribution, revealing heavy-tailed property. Thus, we found two significant properties. First, heavy-ranked attributes are extremely frequent, occurring in almost every schema, whose occurrences tend to dominate in schema matching. Second, tail-ranked attributes rarely occur and are likely unimportant in matching.

However, the rare attributes property poses challenges since they tend to result in overestimated frequency. He *et al.* have addressed this issue by attribute selection and rare attribute smoothing [3, 4]. Besides, Kabra *et al.*[5] have observed that the semantics and relationships between deep web sources are self-revealing by query interfaces, i.e., there are two mutually recursive phenomena: 1) Relevant attributes occur in relevant sources; and 2) Relevant sources contain relevant attributes.

Inspired by observations above, the contributions of this paper are threefold. First, as preprocessing, it proposes an attribute based frequent pattern growth algorithm to extract the most dominant attributes, and a mutual information based approach to capture the relevance. Second, a dominance and relevance based top-k style ranking algorithm is employed to find the top-k data sources on deep web satisfying the user's requirement. Third, extensive experiments are conducted to verify the effectiveness and efficiency of this strategy.

The rest of this paper is organized as follows. Section 2 describes AFP-growth algorithm, while section 3 gives the relevant attributes matrix based on mutual information. Section 4 proposes a novel top-k strategy, and extensive experiments are conducted in section 5. Section 6 describes a summary of related work, and finally section 7 draws the conclusion.

2. AFP-growth Algorithm

According to observations, we know that some attributes are dominant for data sources ranking. Besides, if a source contains many attributes with low relevance, it is probably not of user's interest. Thus, we propose AFP-growth algorithm to mine the most frequent attributes for data sources selection. As preliminary, we apply the following definitions similar to [6].

Definition 1 Let $DS = \{ds_1, ds_2, ..., ds_n\}$ be the set of deep web data sources, and $AS = \{a_1, a_2, ..., a_n\}$ be the set of attributes in DS, given an attribute set $X \subseteq AS$, Sup(X) is defined as the number of data sources containing attributes of X in DS.

Definition 2 Given an attribute set $X \subseteq AS$, we say X is a maximal frequent pattern if X's support is no less than a predefined minimum support threshold min_s, i.e., Sup(X) $\geq min\_s$, and for $\forall (Y \subseteq AS \wedge X \subset Y)$, Sup($Y$)<$min\_s$.

Therefore, given deep web data sources *DS* and a minimum threshold, we can find the most frequent attributes in two steps.

First, we construct an attribute based frequent pattern tree (AFP-tree), where each attribute is specified as a node and the frequent items are dominant attributes. Each node is composed of four parts, with *node_name* and *node_count* specifying the properties, and *node_link* and *node_parent* the two pointers. It creates a frequent item head table *Htable* to traverse the tree, including *item_name* and *item_head*, where the *item_head* points to the first node of the same name in AFP_tree. Details are as follows.

1. Scan the *DS* once , generate frequent attribute set *FA*, calculate Sup(*FA*), sort *FA* in descending order of Sup(*FA*) and get frequent attribute list L_{FA};
2. Create the root of AFP-tree *T*, labeled as "null";
3. For each attribute, sort it according to the order of L_{FA}, specified as {fa_H; fa_L}, where fa_H is the first attribute while fa_L is the list of remaining ones;
4. While fa_L is not null, call insert_tree ({fa_H; fa_L}, *T*), i.e., if there is a node *N* with *node_name*=*p*, then *node_count*(*N*)+1, else create a new node *N*, with *node_name*=*p*, *node_count*(*N*)=1, linked to its parent node *T* by *node_parent* and to the node of the same name by *node_name*.

Second, we propose AFP-growth algorithm, which constructs its AFP-tree, and performs mining recursively. Han *et al.* [6] have demonstrated the efficiency of FP-growth algorithm. Hence, we apply it to our objective.

Algorithm 1: AFP-growth Algorithm

Input: the AFP-tree of *DS*, *min_s*
Output: the Maximal Frequent Attribute Set of *DS*, i.e., MFA(*DS*, *min_s*)

1) MFA=Φ, FA=Φ;   // initialize, FA is the frequent attribute set, FA $\subset$ AS
2) for all $a_i \in AS$ occurring in *DS*, do
3)   MFA[FA]=MFA[FA] $\cup$ { FA $\cup$ { a_i }}
4)   DS'=Φ, Htable=Φ;   //construct DS'
5)   for all $a_j \in AS$ occurring in *DS* such that *j*>*i*, do
6)   if Sup(FA $\cup$ { a_i, a_j })$\geq$ *min_s*, then
7)   Htable=Htable $\cup$ { a_j }
8)   for all (fa_H; fa_L)$\in$ *DS*, with $fa_H \in$ FA do
9)   DS'=DS $\cup$ {FA $\cap$ Htable}
10) Compute MFA(*DS'*, *min_s*)   // depth first recursion
11) MFA(*DS*,*min_s*)=MFA(*DS*,*min_s*) $\cup$ MFA(*DS'*, *min_s*)

---

3. Relevant Attributes Matrix (RAM)

Inspired by the features that relevant attributes occur in relevant sources and relevant sources contain relevant attributes, we employ mutual information to specify the relevance between two dominant attributes based on their co-occurrence, denoted as a Relevant Attributes Matrix (RAM). See definition 3.

Definition 3 Let MFA $= \{a_1, a_2, ..., a_m\}$ be the dominant attributes obtained by AFP-growth algorithm, then Relevant Attributes Matrix (RAM) denoting the relevance of dominant attributes, is defined as:

$$
\text{RAM} = \begin{array}{c} \\ a_1 \\ a_2 \\ \\ a_m \end{array} \begin{array}{cccc} a_1 & a_2 & & a_m \\ \left[mi_{11} \right. & mi_{12} & \cdots & mi_{1m} \\ mi_{21} & mi_{11} & \cdots & \\ \cdots & \cdots & \cdots & \cdots \\ mi_{m1} & mi_{m2} & \cdots & \left. mi_{mn} \right] \end{array} \tag{1}
$$

where,

$$
mi_{ij} = P(a_i, a_j) \log(P(a_i, a_j) / (P(a_i) p(a_j)))
$$

$$
P(a_i, a_j) = C(a_i, a_j) / \sum\nolimits_{a_i', a_j'} C(a_i', a_j') \tag{2}
$$

$$
P(a_i) = C(a_i) / \sum\nolimits_{a_i'} C(a_i')
$$

and $C(a_i, a_j)$ is the frequency of co-occurrences of attributes a_i and a_j within a query interface to the deep web data sources and $\sum_{a_i', a_j'} C(a_i', a_j')$ is that of all the attributes, $C(a_i)$ is the number of occurrence of a_i in the interface and $\sum_{a_i'} C(a_i')$ is that of all the attributes. Therefore, we obtain the mutual information indicating attribute relevance, and generate RAM $= \{mi_{ij}\}_{m \times m}$ denoting the relevance of every two attributes, with mi_{ij} specifying the relevance of a_i to a_j. From formula 2, obviously, we have $mi_{ij} = mi_{ji}$.

Then, the dominance and relevance based top-k style ranking algorithm is proposed, by means of which, the relevant data sources are found with less time cost and thus the efficiency of data sources ranking is improved.

4. Dominance and Relevance based Top-k Style Ranking Algorithm (DR-TRA)

Top-k ranking for the data sources is useful since retrieving too many data sources may be disturbing and the user is probably interested in the top-k results.

Thus, given the deep web data sources and the user's query, our goal is to find the data sources that best satisfy the user's query and to rank them, where we can early terminate the query processing if we find the top-k data sources, without exploiting accesses on all the data sources. Therefore, we propose a dominance and relevance based top-k style ranking algorithm (DR-TRA) by incorporating both the relevance and dominance features of the attributes in deciding which one to probe next to find the relevant data sources, so as to speed up the data sources ranking in exploiting large scale deep web data sources. By using top-k data sources ranking, it does not necessarily access all the data sources and hence with higher efficiency and less time cost.

From section 2, we obtained the sorted list of the dominant attributes, MFA = $\{a_1{}', a_2{}', ..., a_m{}'\}$, and a dominance matrix DM=$\{Nf_{ij}\}_{n \times m}$ for m attributes, n data sources. $Nf_{ij} = Nf(a_i{}', ds_j)$ is the normalized frequency of attribute $a_i{}'$ in data source ds_j. Let dsi_{kj} $(1 < k < s)$ be the interfaces of a data source ds_j, s as the number of query interfaces of data source ds_j, and

$$Nf_{ij} = \sum_{1 < k < s} freq(a_i{}', dsi_{kj})$$
$$freq(a_i{}', dsi_{kj}) = \begin{cases} 1 & sim(a_i{}', dsi_{kj}) \geq \theta \\ 0 & otherwise \end{cases} \quad (3)$$

where $sim(a_i{}', dsi_{kj})$ is the similarity function which evaluates the attribute $a_i{}'$ against the attributes of a data source interface dsi_{kj} of the data source ds_j, and returns a value in the range [0,1], θ a specified threshold.

From section 3, we obtained the relevant attribute matrix RAM based on mutual information approach. Thereby, based on DM and RAM, we develop a combined matrix CM = $\{dr_{ij}\}$, with $dr_{ij} = \sum_{k=1}^{m} (mi_{ik} * Nf_{kj})$ considering both the dominance of an attribute and its relevance with others, and dr_{ij} as the same notation as $dr(a_i{}', ds_j)$, denoting the score of the data source ds_j for the attribute $a_i{}'$. Thus, a top-k ranking algorithm (DR-DRA) is proposed, which employs the Prob-k approach [7] and mainly concerns about what attribute to probe next so that we can drop some unpromising candidates and minimize the query cost. In DR-TRA, we can access on these data sources by matrix CM, where the next probed attribute may not be the next dominant attribute.

Example 1. *For simplicity, we only consider three attributes $\{a_1, a_2, a_3\}$ and three data sources ds_1, ds_2, ds_3. Suppose we have already obtained dominant* *matrix DM from AFP-growth algorithm and RAM based on mutual information, thus we can generate combined matrix CM as follows:*

$$
DM= \begin{array}{c} \\ a_1 \\ a_2 \\ a_3 \end{array} \begin{array}{ccc} ds_1 & ds_2 & ds_3 \\ \begin{bmatrix} 0.9 & 0.7 & 0.6 \\ 0.7 & 0.8 & 0.4 \\ 0.6 & 0.2 & 0.7 \end{bmatrix} \end{array} \quad RAM= \begin{array}{c} \\ a_1 \\ a_2 \\ a_3 \end{array} \begin{array}{ccc} a_1 & a_2 & a_3 \\ \begin{bmatrix} 1 & 0.4 & 0.5 \\ 0.2 & 1 & 0.2 \\ 0.5 & 0.4 & 1 \end{bmatrix} \end{array} \quad CM= \begin{array}{c} \\ a_1 \\ a_2 \\ a_3 \end{array} \begin{array}{ccc} ds_1 & ds_2 & ds_3 \\ \begin{bmatrix} 1.48 & 1.12 & 1.11 \\ 1 & 0.98 & 0.66 \\ 1.33 & 0.87 & 1.16 \end{bmatrix} \end{array}
$$

Thereby we can apply CM to DR-TRA, where attribute a_3 will be second probed.

In DR-TRA, we first sort the data sources according to the most frequent attribute a_1' in descending order, maintain an inverted index list L_i on ds_j, where for each attribute a_i' we keep a list of ordered pairs $(ds_j, dr(a_i',ds_j))$, with $dr(a_i',ds_j)$ corresponding to element dr_{ij} in matrix CM. Then we process a top-k style access on these data sources, which does not necessarily access all the data sources. DR-TRA adopts probabilistic guarantee for those unvisited data sources in evaluating their scores [7, 8], i.e., if the summation of evaluated scores and upper bounds of those unvisited is below a given threshold ε, we can discard it from the candidate set, where each candidate is a data source ds_i that has been visited in at least one list and may qualify for the final top-k result so that we can drop some unpromising candidates and minimize the query cost.

In sum, we find the top-k data sources in two steps. First, as preprocessing, (1) we apply AFP-growth algorithm to selecting the dominant attributes for matching deep web data sources interfaces; (2) relevant attribute matrix RAM of these attributes is generated. Second, based on the combined matrix CM, a top-k style ranking algorithm DR-TRA is applied to ranking relevant data sources without accessing the whole ones, thus the strategy is quite efficient.

Algorithm 2: Top-k Style Ranking Algorithm (DR-TRA)

Input: MFA, threshold ε, DS, k

Output: Top-k Data Sources TDS

1) $TDS=\Phi$; candidates=Φ; $\lambda=0$;   // λ is the threshold for the candidates
2) Repeat   // repeat until retrieving k data sources
3)   for all attribute of MFA the index lists L_j with j=1..m do
4) $dr(ds_{ij})= L_j.getdr()$;   // get the score
5) $E(ds_i)=E(ds_i)\cup \{ ds_i \}$;   // $E(ds_i)$ is the set of evaluated list
           // where ds_i has been visited, initially Φ
6) $high_{ij}= dr(ds_{ij})$; //$high_{ij}$ is upper bound for score of unvisited data sources
7) $worstscore(ds_i)=\sum_{ds_i \in E(ds_i)} dr(ds_i)$

8) $bestscore(ds_i) = worstscore(ds_i) + \sum_{ds_j \in E(ds_i)} high_{ij}$

9)   if $(worstscore(ds_i) > \lambda)$ then

10) $TDS = TDS \cup \{ ds_i \}$;

11)   replace $\min\{worstscore(ds_i') | ds_i' \in TDS\}$ by ds_i'

12)   remove ds_i' from candidates;

13)   else if $(bestscore(ds_i) > \lambda)$ then

14)   candidates = candidates $\cup \{ ds_i \}$;

15)   else drop ds_i from candidates if $ds_i \in$ candidates;

16) $\lambda = \min\{worstscore(ds_i') | ds_i' \in TDS\}$;

17)   for all $ds_i' \in$ candidates do

18)   update $bestscore(ds_i')$ using current $high_{ij}$;

19)   if $(bestscore(ds_i') \leq \lambda$ or $P[bestscore(ds_i') > \lambda] < \varepsilon)$ then

20)   drop ds_i' from candidates;   *// with probabilistic pruning*

21)   if (candidates = Φ or $\max\{bestscore(ds_i') | ds_i' \in$ candidates$\} \leq \lambda$ then

22)   return TDS;   *// early termination*

23)   Until $\|TDS\| = k$

5. Experimental Evaluation

For experimental evaluation, we conducted extensive experiments to evaluate time cost, the precision and recall on the results of top-k data sources with variants of the number of data sources.

5.1. *Datasets and Setup*

We perform our experiments on the datasets *UIUC Web Integration Repository,* which contains 494 Web query interfaces and totally 370 attributes providing information about diverse domains, viz., airfares, automobiles, books, car rentals, hotels, jobs, movies, and music records and is available on-line [9].

     First, we import the data sources we intended for evaluation to an Oracle 10g database. Then, to implement the proposed approaches, we create inverted index lists stored as tables with appropriate indexes to the database. Besides, we generate a hash table for matching the attributes and acquiring the score. All experiments were run on a Pentium® 4 CPU 2.40 GHZ with 512M RAM.

5.2. *Performance Comparisons*

To quantify the evaluation, we test on the deep web repository with different number of data sources and evaluate on three metrics by compare three kinds of top-k approaches, viz., Naïve approach and D-TRA (dominant attributes based top-k ranking) approach, and DR-TRA (dominance and relevance based top-k ranking) approach. Naïve approach is given a query, simply match the attributes of the data source interface to the query, calculate the similarity of each attribute with an IR-style formula and final scores of result data sources with an aggregation function (e.g., sum), then rank the data sources according to final scores. Fig.1 shows the time cost of Naïve approach and that of D-TRA.

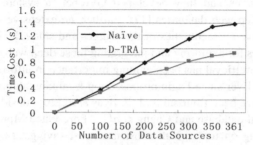

Fig. 1. Time cost of Naïve and D-TRA approach.

Fig.2 and Fig.3 show the precision and recall of the three approaches respectively. We can see that the naïve approach may perform better when the number of data sources is small. However, as the scale of data sources increases, D-TRA approach gradually proves its effectiveness and DR-TRA considering both the dominance and relevance properties of the attributes is the best among three especially the data sources scales.

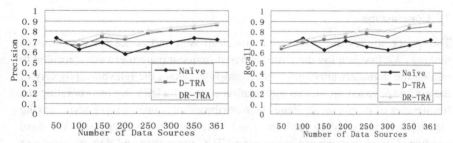

Fig. 2. Precision of Naïve, D-TRA and DR-TRA.   Fig. 3. Recall of Naïve, D-TRA and DR-TRA.

6. Related Work

A wealth of work has been done on deep web research since the rich amount of data sources has gained great attentions recently. To help users find the relevant data sources, many ongoing research efforts, e.g., MetaQuerier [10] and WISE [11], have been conducted on the investigation of large scale deep Web data sources. Raghavan *et al.* [12] proposed HiWe, a task specific crawler for searching deep web while Barbosa *et al.* presented a new crawling strategy to automatically build a deep web directory for locating the data sources[13,14]. Ipeirotis et al. [15, 16] classified contents of text databases by sending probing queries to the sources and they developed QProber, a system for automatic classification of deep web databases [17]. Further, an extensive survey [1] was conducted to observe characteristics of the sources and study the implications of these characteristics for exploring and integrating those deep web databases.

Besides, top-k retrieval has been gaining importance in information retrieval literature [18, 19]. Ever since Fagin proposed top-k ranking algorithm, the top-k style algorithms have been flourishing. I. F. Ilyas *et al.*[20] considered top-k join queries in relational database and Chang *et al.*[21] presented Mpro algorithm for interleaving probing on tuples with substantial cost savings. Marian *et al.*[22] proposed Upper algorithm by adopting an adaptive per-tuple probe scheduling strategy and further developed Whirpool architecture for adaptive processing of top-k queries in XML[23]. Theobald *et al.* developed a probabilistic score prediction technique for early candidate pruning when approximate top-k results is acceptable by the user[8] and further proposed a self-tuning incremental query expansion for top-k query processing [7].

Thus, this paper studies issues for deep web integration and proposes dominance and relevance based top-k algorithm to find relevant data sources.

7. Conclusions

This paper studies the observations on deep web and issues for data sources ranking. We first employ the attribute based frequent pattern growth algorithm to mining the dominant attributes, and meanwhile, obtain the relevance property of the attributes based on mutual information approach. Then, by incorporating the frequencies of dominant attributes with attributes relevance, a top-k style ranking algorithm is proposed to rank the top-k data sources on deep web. We have conducted extensive experiments on the UIUC repository and demonstrated our approach higher efficiency and precision especially in large scale data integration.

References

1.   K. C.-C. Chang, B. He, C. Li, M. Patel, Z. Zhang, Structured databases on the web: Observations and implications, *SIGMOD Record*, 33(3): **61–70** (2004).

2. The deep web: Surfacing hidden value. http://brightplanet.com/ (2006).

3. B. He and K. C.-C. Chang, Statistical schema matching across web query interfaces. In *SIGMOD Conference* (2003).

4. B. He, K. C.-C. Chang, and J. Han, Discovering complex matchings across web query interfaces: A correlation mining approach. In *SIGKDD Conference* (2004).

5. G. Kabra, C.K. Li, C.-C. Chang, Query Routing: Finding Ways in the Maze of the Deep Web. In *Proc. of WIRI* (2005).

6. J. Han, J. Pei, Y. Yin, Mining frequent patterns without candidate generation, ACM Press, **1–12** (2000).

7. M. Theobald, R. Schenkel, G. Weikum, Efficient and Self-tuning Incremental Query Expansion for Top-k Query Processing. In *Proc. of SIGIR*, 2005.

8. M. Theobald, G. Weikum, and R. Schenkel, Top-k query evaluation with probabilistic guarantees. In *Proc. of VLDB*, **648–659** (2004).

9. *UIUC Web Integration Repository*, http://eagle.cs.uiuc. edu/metaquerier.

10. K. C.-C. Chang, B. He, and Z. Zhang, Toward large scale integration: Building a metaquerier over databases on the web. In *CIDR Conference* (2005).

11. H. He, W. Meng, C. Yu, and Z. Wu, Wise-integrator: An automatic integrator of web search interfaces for e-commerce. In *VLDB Conference* (2003).

12. S. Raghavan and H. Garcia-Molina, Crawling the hidden web. In *Proc. of VLDB*, pages **129-138** (2001).

13. L. Barbosa and J. Freire, Siphoning Hidden-Web Data through KeyWord-Based Interfaces. In *Proc. of* SBBD, **309-321** (2004).

14. L. Barbosa and J. Freire, Searching for Hidden-Web Databases. In *Proc. of* WebDB, (2005).

15. P. G. Ipeirotis and L. Gravano, Distributed search over the hidden-web: Hierarchical sampling and selection. In *VLDB* (2002).

16. P. G. Ipeirotis, L. Gravano, and M. Sahami, Probe, count, and classify: Categorizing hidden web databases. In *ACM SIGMOD* (2001).

17. L. Gravano, P. G. Ipeirotis and M. Sahami, QProber, a system for automatic classification of hidden-web databases, *ACM TOIS*, 21(1):**1-41** (2003).

18. R. Fagin, Combining Fuzzy Information from Multiple Systems. In *Proc. of PODS*, (1996).

19. R. Fagin, A. Lotem, and M. Naor, Optimal aggregation algorithms for middleware, *Journal of Computer and System Sciences*, **66: 614-656** (2001).

20. I. F. Ilyas, W. G. Aref, A. K. Elmagarmid, Supporting Top-k Join Queries in Relational Databases, *VLDB* (2003).

21. K. C.-C. Chang, S.-W. Hwang, Minimal Probing: Supporting Expensive Predicates for Top-K Queries, *SIGMOD* (2002).

22. A. Marian, N. Bruno, L. Gravano, Evaluating Top-k Queries over Web-Accessible Databases, *ACM Transactions on Database Systems* (TODS), **29(2)** (2004).

23. A. Marian, A.Y.Sihem et al., Adaptive Processing of Top-k Queries in XML. In *Proc. of ICDE* (2005).

AUTOMATED WEB SERVICE DISCOVERY

LEV SHULMAN[A], ELIAS IOUP[A], JOHN SAMPLE[B], KEVIN SHAW[B]
and MAHDI ABDELGUERFI[A]

[A]*Computer Science Department, University of New Orleans*
New Orleans, LA 70148, USA

[B]*Mapping, Charting, and Geodesy, Naval Research Laboratory*
Stennis Space Center, MS 39529, USA

As Web Services become increasingly important so do the portals that index the services. Common portal of Web Services require publishing to the registry. While manually compiled registries are useful, they often fail to include a large number of Web Services available for public use. Rather than require a Web Service operator to publish to a registry or catalog, we propose to create an automated discovery system which finds and indexes Web Services within a particular application. By using a combination of directed search and web crawling we are able to find a large number of candidate sites which can be validated and added to a portal. Results show that our method is successful in discovering large number of Geospatial Web Services and is better than the methods which rely solely on directed search.

1. Introduction

During the last several years, there has been a tremendous growth in the number of Web Services publicly available on the web, from a variety of fields such as eCommerce, finance, banking, digital libraries, online news media, and geographical information services. Web Service Portals or Catalogs have arisen to provide the user with a single access point, or index, from which to search and browse for Web Services of interest. However, for the number of sources indexed by such a portal to grow, Web Service providers must either publish their services to such a portal, or new services must be manually discovered on the web and integrated into a portal system.

By taking advantage of Web Services that adhere to well-defined open standards, we present the design and implementation of a Web Service Portal System that is fully capable of search, discovery, and integration of Web Services in a fully automated manner using scalable web crawling techniques. While the brute force method of validating every possible HTTP URL to a web service schema would discover all possible Web Services, such an approach is obviously untenable. The resources required to crawl the entire web are out of scale for all but the largest systems. Instead, an intelligent method of selecting URLs which are more likely to lead to a valid web service is necessary. By using domain knowledge to lead our search, the number of possible HTTP URLs to test is greatly reduced allowing the crawling process to be viable.

For this research, we focus on Geospatial Web Services. Geospatial data is often most useful when combined together, leading to a large availability of geospatial services available for public use. The usefulness of combining disparate geospatial services provides a large impetus for a unified access portal which discovers and indexes the services available on the Internet.

This paper is organized as follows. First, some background is presented on Web Services in general, Geospatial Web Service standards, and current Geospatial portals. Second, we discuss the use of the Google API to produce a set of domain appropriate seed URLs which are then crawled to create a set of candidate URLs to be validated. Third is a description of the validation process for these URLs, in this case validation to the Open GIS Consortium Web Mapping Service standard, and their inclusion into a unified Web Mapping Service Portal. Finally, some results are presented which show the effectiveness of our method in comparison to an alternate technique.

2. Background

2.1. *Web Services*

A Web Service is an Application Programmatic Interface (API) written as an XML document that validates to an XML Schema. The common standard for such a document validates to a Web Service Definition Language Schema [1]. We will call a Web Service domain a collection of published Web Services that validate to a common standard WSDL Schema, and formulate the problem addressed in this paper: how to automatically find and bind to Web services within a particular Web Service domain, given a WSDL schema for that domain? For example, several online newspaper providers such as the Washington Post, the New York Times, and the Houston Chronicle each provide a Web Service for user applications to bind to and retrieve news feeds on a daily basis. Each newspaper's Web Service is an XML document that validates to a common WSDL schema. With automatic discovery and integration, a portal system in the online newspaper domain could be programmed to automatically finds and integrate Web Services from other online news Web Services that validate to the same WSDL schema.

2.2. OGC Geospatial Web Services

Geospatial Web Services are often provided using a separate standard created by the Open Geospatial Consortium (OGC). The OGC provides public XML schemas for a variety of Web Services such as the Web Mapping Service (WMS), Web Feature Service (WFS), and Web Coverage Service (WCS) [2]. The OGC Web Services paradigm is analogous to its SOAP/WSDL counterpart, in that an OGC Web Service provides an XML Document that consists of service interface descriptions, along with the details of their bindings. This document, called a Capabilities document by the OGC, serves as an API used to generate server and client code and validates to a public standard XML schema published by the OGC. A client retrieves and scans this document to issue requests for geospatial layers featured within the document.

Although the approach described in this paper applies to all OGC Web Services as well as Web Services employing the SOAP/WSDL model, this research focuses mainly on the Web Mapping Service. The WMS specification defines an interface to server applications that provide map images [3]. The benefit of focusing only on the Web Mapping Service is the prevalence of open data sources and the desire to have comprehensive listings of these data sources.

A WMS server is most often advertised by a typical HTTP URL such as http://www.wmsServerHost.com/path. Requests to the WMS server are constructed by configuring key-value pairs in the query part of the URL, for example, a URL of the form http://www.wmsServerHost.com/path? REQUEST=GetCapabilities&SERVICE=WMS. This URL should return an XML Capabilities document that adheres to a WMS Capabilities schema as published by the Open Geospatial Consortium. The Capabilities document describes the map layers that the WMS Server provides, along with the WMS server's contact info and metadata.

Fetching a map from a WMS server can be as simple as typing a WMS URL request in an internet browser to retrieve the image. For example, http://dmap.nrlssc.navy.mil/ogcwms/servlet/WMSServlet/GIDBImageServer.w ms?REQUEST=GetMap&SERVICE=WMS&LAYERS=NASA_BLUE& BBOX=-180.0,-90.0,180.0,90.0&WIDTH=800&HEIGHT=600&FORMAT= image/png. This HTTP URL returns a NASA Blue Marble PNG map image of 800 pixels width and 600 pixel height for the geographic region bounded by -180° and 180° longitude and -90° and 90° latitude. The WMS server host is "dmap.nrlssc.navy.mil", and the URL path is "/ogcwms/servlet/WMSServlet/ GIDBImageServer.wms?". The various map request parameters in the query part of the URL, "REQUEST=GetMap&SERVICE=WMS&LAYERS=

NASA_BLUE&BBOX=-180.0,-90.0,180.0,90.0&WIDTH=800&HEIGHT= 600&FORMAT=image/png" are simple HTTP key-value pairs that specify the geometric bounding box of the map image, pixel width and height, etc.. There are a number of user-friendly WMS client applications that provide a variety of mapping capabilities such as zoom in/out, map image transparency, layering, etc., by configuring the HTTP key-value pairs according to user actions.

2.3. *Previous Work*

Work on discovery of Web Services is fairly limited. Currently, Web Services are often included portals or catalogs that require manual entry or registration. For Web Services described by WSDL documents, UDDI is the standard registry. For Geospatial Web Services, the OGC defines a Catalog Service but most registries are adhoc creations such as the US Geological Survey's National Map [4] and the National Spatial Data Infrastructure Clearing-house portal [5].

Automatic discovery of Geospatial Web Services have been investigated by a few groups. The first is the Refractions Research OGC Survey [6]. They use the Google API to search the Internet for possible OGC Web Services. The Google Search API is used to find URLs which contain the query string for a OGC Capabilities document. Using this approach they achieve a high probability that any results they find will provide an OGC Web Service. However, many sites do not publish the links to their capabilities documents and will be undiscoverable using this method. The Mapdex map server index [7] uses a similar Google API search method to find both standards based Web Mapping Services as well as the non-standard ArcIMS Mapping Services (a commonly used proprietary solution similar to WMS). An alternate technique is provided by Skylab Mobilesystems [8] which uses a form of Web crawling to discover Web Mapping Services. They details of their crawling system are not published, however, their WMS Server list is not extensive, consisted in large part of WMS sources provided by our portal.

3. Web Service Discovery

While the number of available WMS Servers on the web has been growing steadily, searching for new WMS sources is often reduced to simply "googling" to find WMS Servers on the internet. Automating this process has led to the Google API search method employed by Refractions Research. They use the Google APIs to search for WMS Capabilities documents. A WMS Server's "Capabilities" document may be retrieved by constructing a URL of the form:

http://wmsServerHost/path?REQUEST=GetCapabilities

The Refractions Research queries Google with strings such as "url:REQUEST=GetCapabilities" in the Google API search query. The Google API query returns URLs of this form which are then processed to verify whether a URL returns a valid OGC Web Service Capabilities document. However, WMS Servers may be advertised on the internet by simply providing its WMS Server URL, such as http://wmsServerHost/path, without the "REQUEST= GetCapabilities&SERVICE=WMS" appended. Consider a website that hosts a spreadsheet or xml listing of WMS Servers advertised this way. None of the servers would be found using the Google APIs approach above, for there is no URL pattern substring pattern to take advantage of. In addition, there may be sites on the web advertising WMS sources that are simply not indexed by Google.

We have devised an automated approach to discovering Web Services such as WMS sources by reformulating the problem and considering the following assertions:

- Every WMS Server has a published XML document that validates to a common XML schema as published by the Open Geospatial Consortium.
- Every WMS Server will return a valid OGC WMS Capabilities Document when issued a HTTP GET to its URL with the Capabilities query string attached.

By approaching the problem as one of validation instead of search we are able to improve upon the simple Google Search API method of discovery. Because validating the set of all HTTP URLs is untenable, we propose to filter the set of all URLs to include only those most likely to be a Web Mapping Service. The best filter would be one which only returns sites in our Web Service domain, in this case Geospatial Web Services. For this purpose, we combine both the Google Search API with a web crawler.

The Web crawler is employed to gather a set of WMS URLs from within a particular domain or hop range. For example, using the crawler with http://www.opengis.org as the seed URL will likely find several WMS Servers. The total number of web sites collected by the crawler for validation is small but the probability of finding WMS Servers is high. Because it is important to seed the Web crawler with URLs which have a high probability of returning appropriate Web Services, the task becomes finding seed URLs related to the Web Service domain of the target Web Services. The Google Search API is well suited to this task. Searching for strings such as "WMS Maps" and "OpenGIS Web Services" with the Google Search API returns a list of seed URLs relevant to this Web Service domain. These URLs are then fed into the web crawler which will collect a larger list of URLs to be validated later. The performance of the Web crawler is improved by ignoring all URLs that return irrelevant HTTP MIME header types such as images, video streams, executables, etc. However, the Web crawler is intelligent about detecting embedded URLs in many different data types including HTML, XML, Word files, Excel files, and raw binary sources. Our approach has benefits over those that rely on solely the Google Search API because it will find WMS Servers whose URLs do not include the query string for the Capabilities Document, the basis for a WMS Google search. For example, the WMS servers provided at http://mesonet.agron.iastate.edu do not append query strings to the end of their URLs. The Refractions Research crawler fails to find these WMS servers, whereas our discovery system does.

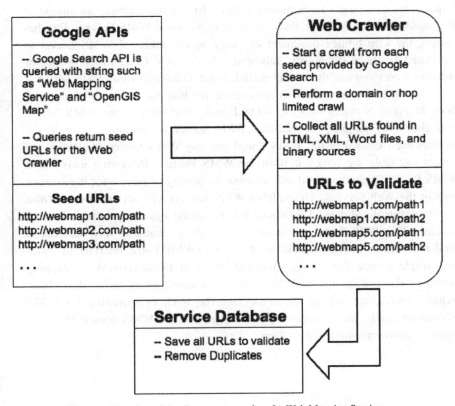

Figure 1: Overview of the discovery procedure for Web Mapping Services.

4. Validation and Portal Integration

The Web crawler compiles a set of URLs to validate as Web Mapping Services. These URLs are placed inside a database for later validation. All URLs saved in the database are unique; checks ensure that duplicates are not added. Once the crawler adds a URL to the database the validation component will detect if it represents an actual Web Mapping Service. Every WMS Server must correctly respond to a request for its Capabilities document which is made by sending an HTTP GET request to the URL with the query string "REQUEST=GetCapabilities&SERVICE=WMS" appended to it. The response should be an XML document which validates to the schema document published by the OGC. Thus, every URL compiled by the crawler will be saved as a valid WMS source only if it responds to the Capabilities query with a valid Capabilities document. Even though WMS URLs in the database are unique, it is possible for two different URLs to refer to the same WMS Server. For this reason, the Capabilities document of every newly validated WMS Server is compared to those previously validated. If the new Capabilities document matches a previous one then the new URL is not added as a valid WMS Server.

The WMS Driver system is responsible for binding the newly discovered Web Mapping Services into the WMS Portal. Periodically, the WMS Driver will check the database of validated WMS Server for changes. New WMS Servers are included in the WMS Portal and any WMS Servers which are no longer available are removed from the WMS Portal. Removing unavailable WMS Servers from the portal will increase the quality of service for the average user of the Web Service. Unavailable WMS Servers will not be removed from the database of validated URLs and will be added again once they return to service. The WMS Portal acts as an index to all the available Web Services as well as a unified interface to access them. The WMS Portal interface provides one single source for all data indexed from all discovered Web Mapping Services. By configuring the WMS Portal as a single interface to all available WMS sources, the system saves the user the work of searching for WMS Servers manually, and provides access to a vast array of WMS content from one comprehensive mapping application.

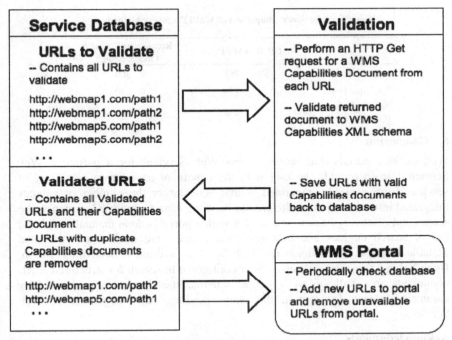

Figure 2: Overview of the process of validating possible WMS Server URLs and integrating them into the WMS Portal.

5. Results

The WMS Crawler, WMS Driver, and WMS Portal are currently integrated into the Geographic Information Database™ (GIDB) hosted at http://dmap.nrlssc.navy.mil [9]. The approach for automated discovery and integration of Web Mapping Services used by the WMS Portal Crawler in GIDB has tangible benefits over simpler methods employed by groups such as Refractions Research. Table 1 shows a comparison between the GIDB WMS Crawler and the Refractions Research Google API Search (all references to WMS Servers provided by GIDB have been removed). The GIDB WMS Crawler found more than three times as many WMS Servers and thirty-four more unique serving hosts. A unique host may provide multiple Web Mapping Services. Based on the ratio between WMS Servers and unique hosts, the GIDB WMS Crawler is much more successful than Refractions Research at finding multiple WMS Servers on one host. This result makes sense since the GIDB WMS Crawler will search through all linked documents in a particular domain whereas Refractions Research will only test the single host returned by a Google Search.

Table 1. Performance comparison of WMS Discovery Methods.

	GIDB WMS Crawler	Refractions Research Google Search
WMS Servers	761	309
Unique Hosts	174	140
Servers Uniquely Found By Method	436	84

6. Conclusion

Web Service portals that broker access Web Services for a particular Web Service domain provide the user with the benefit of access to a vast array of services from a single integrated source. The larger the number of sources integrated into such a portal, the greater its value is as a service. Commonly, the search and discovery of new sources for such a portal is done manually with the use of search engines and catalogs. Instead, we have created an automated scalable solution which discovers Web Services without manual intervention. By utilizing a topic driven web crawler configured to search for structured XML documents that validate to a public schema, the system contains a fully automated means for search, discovery, binding, and integration of Web Services.

Acknowledgments

This research was partially funded by the Office of Naval Research.

References

1. Web Services Description Language (WSDL) Version 2.0 Part 0: Primer. March 2006. http://www.w3.org/TR/wsdl20-primer/.
2. Open Geospatial Consortium Specifications. November 2006. http://www.opengeospatial.org/standards/
3. J. Beaujardiere, "Web Map Service Implementation Specifications, Version 1.3," Aug. 2004; http://portal.opengeospatial.org/files/index.php?artifact_id -5316.
4. Katherine Brown. "Digital Information Systems: Mapping the Future." Science, 2002 Dec. 6;298 (5600):1874-5.
5. National Spatial Data Infrastructure Portal. http://geodata.gov/
6. Refractions Research OGC Survey. http://www.refractions.net/white_papers/-ogcsurvey/, October 2006.
7. Mapdex. http://mapdex.org
8. Skylabs Mobisystems OGC Server List. http://www.skylab-mobilesystems.com/en/wms_serverlist.html
9. John T. Sample, Roy Ladner, Lev Shulman, Elias Ioup, Fred Petry, Elizabeth Warner, Kevin Shaw, Frank P. McCreedy, "Enhancing the US Navy's GIDB Portal with Web Services," IEEE Internet Computing, vol. 10, no. 5, pp. 53-60, Sept/Oct, 2006.

VISUAL MEDIA DATA RETRIEVAL BASED ON
WEB SERVICE MATCHMAKING[*]

SEONG-WOO LEE, CHULBUM AHN, BOWON SUH,
O-BYOUNG KWON and YUNMOOK NAH

Department of Electronics and Computer Engineering,
Dankook University, Seoul, Korea
{swlee, bwsuh, obkwon}@dblab.dankook.ac.kr, {ahn555, ymnah}@dku.edu

With the rapid increase of Web Service sites, one emerging problem is how to find most appropriate Services among massive number of similar Web Services and another problem is how to overcome the heterogeneity of metadata among them. In this paper, we propose intelligent service finding techniques for the HERMES, which is a Web Service-enabled visual media retrieval framework. We show how Semantic Web technology can be utilized to find appropriate visual media Web Services. We also propose how metadata can be transformed to overcome the heterogeneity among visual media Web Services.

1. Introduction

With the wide spread use of digital image capturing devices, such as scanner, digital camera and camera phone, the amount of visual media, including image and video, on the internet is ever increasing rapidly. A number of research groups have been exploring different approaches for searching image data by title, content, or semantic meaning. Earlier and most of current image database systems and image search engines usually support image searching by simply using descriptive formatted data, such as caption and title. During the last decade, many content-based image retrieval (CBIR) or semantic contents-based image retrieval techniques have been studied widely. The pioneering work has been done by IBM's QBIC (Query By Image Content) system, which supports queries using color, shape, sketch, and texture features on images, such as post stamps, art pictures, and trademark drawings [1]. The Chabot system was another interesting CBIR system, with high level concepts, such as 'light yellow' and 'sunset,' as well as low level features based on color [2]. One of the most recent research work has been done by the SIMPLIcity system which supports image searching based on the color, texture, shape features, while increasing matching correctness by utilizing local features on regions [3]. In the

[*] This research was supported by the Ministry of information and Communication, Korea, under the College Information Technology Research Center Support Program, grant number IITA-2006-C1090-0603-0031.

medical domain, the KMeD(Knowledge-Based Medical Database) system utilizes semantic modeling focusing on object shapes and spatial relationships between them [4,5]. We developed NERD-IDB, which supports the meaning-based retrieval on neuroscience image databases [6]. We also proposed web catalog image retrieval system, which support intelligent retrieval using keyword, color, texture features and high-level concepts [7,8].

Web Services are a standardized way of integrating Web-based applications using open standards including XML, the SOAP(Simple Object Access Protocol), the WSDL(Web Service Description Language), and the UDDI(Universal Description, Discovery, and Integration) specification. XML structures the message, SOAP transfers the message, WSDL describes the available services, and UDDI list them. XML describes both the nature of each self-contained function and the data that flows among systems [9]. The CPXe, proposed by Eastman Kodak, is a Web Service driven photo marketing system, but this system supports simple keyword-based searching only and does not utilize semantics [10]. The SOTA is an ontology-mediated Web Service system for smart office task automation [11]. The previously developed image databases, such as QBIC, Chabot, NERD-IDB, etc, can be considered as image service providers from the viewpoint of Web Services. With the rapid increase of such Web Service sites, one emerging problem is how to find most appropriate Services among massive number of similar Web Services and another problem is how to overcome the heterogeneity of Web Services, each of them using different metadata formats.

In our previous research, we proposed an architecture, called the *HERMES*(tHE Retrieval framework for visual MEdia Service), which is a Web Service-enabled visual media retrieval framework, consisting of HERMES/B node (Web Service broker) and multiple HERMES/P nodes (Web Service providers), each servicing their own visual media resources [12]. In this paper, we propose intelligent Service finding techniques for the HERMES. The major purpose of this paper is: 1) to show how Web Service and Semantic Web technologies can be utilized to find appropriate Web Services and 2) to present how the heterogeneity among Web Service sites can be overcome by metadata mapping.

The remainder of this paper is organized as follows. Section 2 describes overview of Web Service, Semantic Web, metadata, and the visual media service architecture. Section 3 explains the service finding techniques, including ontology-enabled query extension, metadata mapping, and Web Service-based matchmaking. In section 4, we describe our current prototype system. Finally, section 5 concludes the paper.

2. Overview of Visual Media Service Architecture

In this section, we briefly review the overall architecture of the visual media service framework. The architecture named the HERMES is a Web Service-enabled visual media retrieval framework architecture, which consists of HERMES/B node and multiple HERMES/P nodes, each servicing visual media resources using their own metadata standard format or customized metadata format. F.E.S (Feature Extraction Service) Providers provide local and/or global feature extraction services. The HERMES/B, HERMES/Ps and clients communicate with each other using XML messages.

The HERMES/B takes a role of Web Service broker from the point of Web Service, a meta-searcher from the viewpoint of information retrieval, and intelligent agent from the viewpoint of intelligent information systems. Figure 1 shows the detail architecture of HERMES/B. The Query Handler receives user queries, reformulates queries using metadata and broker ontology, and sends the reformulated queries to HERMES/Ps. The Query Processor transforms query string into provider-specific XML queries. The Query Result Integrator combines query results and sends them back to users. The Matchmaker finds best service provider list for the given query. The Service Inference Engine determines service provider list by using Service Ontology and Service Registry. The Metadata Mapping Manager transforms query string into provider-specific format by using Metadata Registry. The Service Registration Handler registers services provided by HERMES/Ps. Provider-specific service and metadata information are stored in Service Registry and Metadata Registry. The Feature Handler selects suitable F.E.S. Providers and/or obtains features using them.

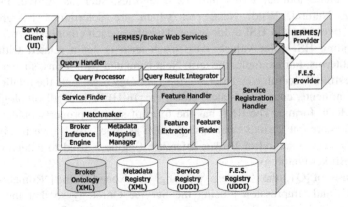

Figure 1. HERMES Broker architecture (adapted from [12]).

HERMES/P consists of modules, such as Query Processor, Visual Media Manager, Provider Inference Engine, Semantic Metadata Manager, Visual Media Search Engine, Provider Registration Handler, and Semantic Annotator [12]. Service Client provides fill-in query forms, in which users can specify Service Domain, Author, Title, Subject, Creation Date, Description, Emotion, Color, and Location information, which are used as search criteria. The example query forms can be found in section 4.

3. Visual Media Service Finding

The representative sample queries are as follows: find 'modern painting' images whose creator is 'Albers' (Q1), find 'peaceful' images whose creator is 'Beauneveu' (Q2) and find photos of 'Californian' nature (Q3). All these queries require ontology-based Service site matchmaking and metadata mapping.

To find the most appropriate Services, the Broker Inference Engine extends service domains by using Broker Specific Ontology, the Matchmaker finds Web Services using the extend service domains and ranks Services using information on Service sites in Service Registry, and finally the Metadata Mapping Manager transforms the HERMES/B metadata into provider-specific metadata.

3.1. *Ontology-enabled Query Extension*

Broker Ontology consists of Service Ontology, Emotion Ontology and Location Ontology. The *Service Ontology* classifies the visual media service domain. For example, Image is classified into Art, Medical, and Photo; Photo is again classified into Human, Plant, Life, Animal, Nation, Vehicle, Scenery, etc. The *Emotion Ontology*, which is built from our previous research result [13], classifies the emotional terms into 12 categories, such as Active, Positive, Sparkling, Natural, Wild, Neat, etc, which are determined by grouping representative colors in HSI color space. Therefore, each emotional term has its corresponding HSI color values. Also, each term is again related with other emotional terms. For example, the term Neat is related with terms, such as Cool, Clean, Restful, Peaceful, etc. The *Location Ontology* represents the relationships among continents, countries, states, cities, etc. In HERMES, all ontologies are stored in RDF format. The RDF has the form of subject-property-object which can easily represent various relationships such as 'is-a'. As shown in Figure 2, the InferQuery( ) method of Broker Inference Engine is used to extend queries by using Broker Ontology.

In case of Q1, the 'modern painting' is expanded to {'Romanticism', 'Realistic', and 'Impression'} using the Service Ontology so that the search engine can easily match the target images. In case of Q2, the emotional term 'peaceful' is changed to corresponding HSI color values by using the Emotion Ontology. In case of Q3, we need Service Ontology to find sites related with image, photo and scenery and Location Ontology to further expand the location 'California' to 'Los Angeles', 'Orange County', etc.

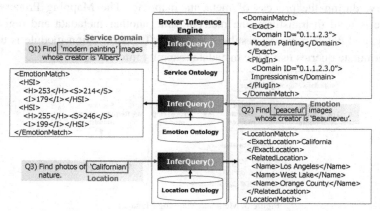

Figure 2. Query extension by Broker Inference Engine (for Q1, Q2, Q3).

3.2. *Metadata Mapping to Overcome Heterogeneity*

Each metadata standard can use different element name for the exactly same element. For example, the element 'Creator' in DC standard is tagged by the element 'Creator Name' in VRA standard. There exist semantic heterogeneities among metadata from the semantic, structural and syntactic viewpoints as shown in Table 1.

Table 1. Types of metadata mapping.

Type	Type Name	Example
Semantic	direct-substitution	Creator –> CreatorName
	indirect-substitution	Identifier –> IDnumber
	is-a	Creator –> Person, Corperate
	part-whole	Title –> MainTitle, SubTitle
Structural	composition	FirstName, LastName –> Name
	decomposition	Name –> FirstName, LastName
Syntactic	code set	ISO 6093 –> ISO 8601
	data type	String –> Date, Integer –> Float

The Metadata Mapping Manager is used to handle these problems. The internal structure of Metadata Mapping Manager is shown in Figure 3. The MDR Search module is used to retrieve, store, update, delete metadata mapping information from/to Metadata Registry. Metadata Registry of HERMES/B consists of Provider Schema table, Mapping table and MDR Standard table.

Provider Schema table stores provider-specific metadata information, MDR Standard table stores standard metadata information and Mapping table stores mapping information between metadata formats. The Service Registry Search module is used to get information on Web Service providers from the Service Registry, during the process of metadata mapping. The Mapping Processing module is used to transform one metadata into another metadata and register, modify, and delete mapping results. The Query Transformation module is used to reformulate queries using the metadata mapping information.

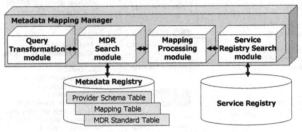

Figure 3. Metadata Mapping Manager.

The Metadata Mapping Manager can provide mapping between HERMES/B standard metadata (called common metadata), which is DC standard in our current implementation, and other HERMES/P standard metadata (called provider-specific metadata), as shown in Figure 4.

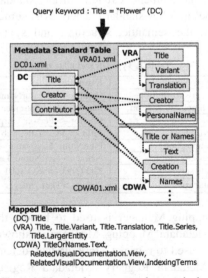

Figure 4. Mapping between metadata standards.

The CustomizeQuery() method of the Query Transformation module transforms the HERMES/B metadata to the HERMES/P metadata and the RestoreQueryResult() method transforms the HERMES/P metadata to HERMES/B metadata, as shown in Figure 5.

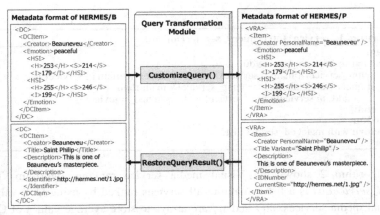

Figure 5. Query reformulation by the Metadata Mapping Manager (for Q2).

3.3. *Web Service Matchmaking and Ranking*

The Matchmaker of HERMES/B is used to find the Service providers for a given query. For this purpose, it utilizes information stored in the Service Registry. The Service Registry is a UDDI. Therefore, it contains general UDDI entries, such as ProviderKey, ProviderName, ProviderDescription, Contact, ServiceKey, ServiceName, ServiceDescription, ServiceURL (access point URL for connection to a Service), and OverviewDocURL (WSDL document URL of a Service). It also contains the extended entries which are defined for the HERMES by using tModel. The typical QoS elements, such as Cost, Time, Reliability, Accuracy, Availability, and LastUpdateTime, are adopted from [14] and [15]. The remaining entries, such as NumOfMedia, Metadata, and MediaQuality, are added for visual media Services. To find appropriate Web Services, the service domain names extended by the Broker Inference Engine are compared to the ServiceDomain element of the Service Registry UDDI. The matched Services are stored in the array variable ServiceList.

Algorithm 1 shows the Visual media service matching algorithm. The *query_serviceDomain* means service domain extracted from user query and the *temp_serviceDomain* is a temporary variable which saves service domain of each service. *num_of_service* is the number of all services in Service Registry(UDDI) and *serviceList* is a list containing all services in service registry. *matched_serviceList* is a list containing all services matched exactly with the *query_serviceDomain*. To rank the Web Services, the standard t-scores (TSs) [16] upon each of the QoS entries are computed.

Algorithm 1. serviceMatch(query_serviceDomain)
```
begin
  for i=1 to num_of_service do
      temp_serviceDomain = serviceDomain of ith serviceItem in serviceList;
      if query_serviceDomain = temp_serviceDomain then
          add ith serviceItem in serviceList to matched_sercviceList;
      endif
  endfor
  return with matched_serviceList;
end
```

Algorithm 2 shows the Visual media service ranking algorithm. The *ranked_serviceList* is a list containing all services ranked by using QoS values of visual media services. *m[]* and *s[]* are arrays to store average values of QoS elements of all serviceItems in matched_serviceList and T-score values, respectively. *Sum_QoS_value* means total sum of QoS weights.

Algorithm 2. serviceRank(matched_serviceList, QoSWeight)
```
begin
  for i=1 to num_of_service do
     replace values of all QoS elements of ith serviceItem in matched_serviceList
     by new value to calculate T-score;
  endfor
  for i=1 to 10 do
      calculate average of ith QoS element value of all serviceItem in
      matched _serviceList; assign the average to m[i];
  endfor
  for i=1 to 10 do
    calculate s for T-score of ith QoS element;   assign s to s[i];
  endfor
  for i=1 to num_of_service do
     for i=1 to 10 do
        calculate T-score of jth QoS element of ith serviceItem using jth
        QoSWeight, m[j] an s[j];
     endfor
     assign total T-score of all QoS elements of ith serviceItem to rankingPoint of
     ith serviceItem; add ith serviceItem to ranked_serviceList;
  endfor
  sort serviceItems in serviceList by rankingPoint of serviceItem;
  return with ranked_serviceList;
end
```

4. Prototype Implementation

We developed the prototype system using a computer equipped with a Pentium IV/Xeon 2.8GHz CPU and 1Gbyte main memory on .NET platform of the Windows 2003 server. To save and register visual media services, we used Microsoft UDDI registry. Total system is composed of one HERMES/B node and ten HERMES/P nodes which provide visual media services.

Figure 6 shows the execution snapshot of example query (Q2) in our current prototype of HERMES. The query forms and results for Q1 and Q3 are similar to Figure 6. The pull-down list and fill-in boxes on the left side of the window is the query interface of HERMES. The Service Domain is specified by selecting the pull-down list. This domain information is provided by the HERMES/B to the Service Client. When user clicks the Search button, the HERMES shows the Service Provider information, which is shown in the shaded rectangle on the right side, and the retrieved results from the Service Provider, in the order of ranking of Service Providers.

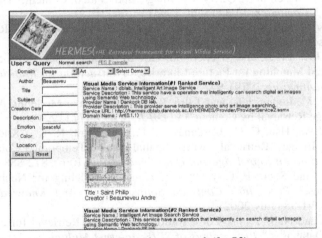

Figure 6. Example query result (for Q2).

5. Conclusion

In this paper, we proposed web service finding techniques for distributed visual media retrieval. We showed how Web Service and Semantic Web technologies can be utilized to find appropriate Web Services and presented how the heterogeneity among Web Services can be solved by metadata mapping. The service finding techniques, including query extension using broker ontology, query reformulation through metadata mapping, and Web Service-based matchmaking and ranking, are described. The messages transferred among HERMES nodes and among internal HERMES components are all structured in XML form. We also described the overall query processing sequence of Web Service Broker.

We are currently developing the prototype of the HERMES architecture, but the detail or optimal algorithms of each component should be further developed. We will construct further ontologies to support other visual media, such as video and other visual media domains. We believe that experimental studies on the performance aspects are highly meaningful subjects for future research. To improve the performance, we plan to devise client-side caching strategies to speed up the Web Service message transfer and introduce the load balancing and fault-tolerance schemes into HERMES/B.

References

1. Flickner, M. et al., "Query by Image and Video Content: The QBIC System," *Computer.* 23-32 (Sept. 1995).
2. Ogle, V.E. and Stonebraker, M., "Chabot: Retrieval from a Relational Database of Images," *Computer.* 40-48 (Sept. 1995).
3. Wang, J.Z., Li, J., and Wiederhold, G., "SIMPLIcity: Semantics-Sensitive Integrated Matching for Picture Libraries," *Transactions on Knowledge and Data Engineering*, 23(9). 947-963 (2001).
4. Chu, W.W., Leong, I.T., and Taira, R.K., "A Semantic Modeling Approach for Image Retrieval by Content," *VLDB J.*, 3. 445-477 (1994).
5. Chu, W.W., Hsu, C.-C., Cardenas, A. F., and Taira, R. K., "Knowledge-Based Image Retrieval with Spatial and Temporal Constructs," *Transactions on Knowledge and Data Engineering*, 10(6). 872-888 (1998).
6. Nah, Y. and Sheu, P. C.-y., "Image Content Modeling for Neuroscience Databases," *Proc. Int'l Conf. on Software Eng. And Knowledge Eng. (SEKE)*. 91-98 (July 2002).
7. Lee, B. and Nah, Y., "A Color Ratio based Image Retrieval for e-Catalog Image Databases," *Proceedings of SPIE: Internet Multimedia Management Systems II*, Vol. 4519. 97-105 (August 2001).
8. Hong, S., Lee, C., and Nah, Y., "An Intelligent Web Image Retrieval System," *Proceedings of SPIE: Internet Multimedia Management Systems II*, Vol. 4519. 106-115 (August 2001).
9. Chung, J.-Y., Lin, K.-J. and Mathieu, R. G., "Web Services Computing: Advancing Software Interoperability," *Computer*, 36(10). 35-37 (Oct. 2003).
10. Thompson, T., Weil, R. and Wood M. D., "CPXe: Web Services for Internet Imaging," *Computer*, 36(10). 54-62 (Oct. 2003).

11. Tsai, T.M., Yu, H.-K., et al., "Ontology-Mediated Integration of Intranet Web Services," *Computer*, 36(10). 63-71 (Oct. 2003).
12. Nah, Y., Lee, B. and Kim, J., "Visual Media Retrieval Framework using Web Service," LNCS, 3597, 104-113 (July 2005).
13. Hong, S., Ahn, C., Nah, Y. and Choi, L., "Searching Color Images by Emotional Concepts," LNCS, 3597, 361-365 (July 2005).
14. Cardoso, J. and Sheth, A., "Semantic e-Workflow Composition," *J. of Intelligent Information Systems* (2002).
15. Mani, A. and Nagarajan, A., "Understanding quality of service for Web Services," http://www-106.ibm.com/developerworks/library/ws-quality. html?n-ws-1172 (2002) .
16. You, S.-Y., Yu, J.-Y. and Lee, K.-C., "QoS Matching Mechanism for Semantic Web Service," *Proc. KISS Spring Conference* (April 2004).

A PRELIMINARY STUDY ON THE EXTRACTION
OF SOCIO-TOPICAL WEB KEYWORDS

KULWADEE SOMBOONVIWAT

Graduate School of Information Science and Technology, University of Tokyo,
7-3-1 Hongo, Bunkyo-ku, Tokyo, 113-0033, Japan
E-mail: kulwadee@tkl.iis.u-tokyo.ac.jp

SHINJI SUZUKI

Institute of Industrial Science, University of Tokyo,
4-6-1 Komaba, Meguro-ku, Tokyo, 153-8505, Japan
E-mail: suzuki@tkl.iis.u-tokyo.ac.jp

MASARU KITSUREGAWA

Institute of Industrial Science, University of Tokyo,
4-6-1 Komaba, Meguro-ku, Tokyo, 153-8505, Japan
E-mail: kitsure@tkl.iis.u-tokyo.ac.jp

In recent years, the Web has become a popular medium for disseminating information, news, ideas, and opinions of the modern society. Due to this phenomenon, the Web information is reflecting current events and trends that are happening in the real world which, in turn, has attracted a lot of interest in using the Web as a sociological research tool for detecting the emerging topics, and social trends. To facilitate such kind of sociological research, in this paper, we study the characteristics of socio-topical web keywords sampled from a series of Thai web snapshots. The socio-topical web keyword, extracted from the content of some web pages, is a keyword relating to some topics of interest in a real-world society. The study was conducted as follows. First, the socio-topical keywords were sampled from the inverted index of each Thai web snapshot. Then, for each sampled keyword, we observe the pattern of changes of the number of documents containing the keyword, and the inverse document frequency (IDF) scores. Finally, we try to find the relationships between the observed patterns of changes and their corresponding real-world events in the Thai society.

1. Introduction

The Web has been increasingly gaining popularity as a tool for disseminating information, news, ideas, and opinions of the modern society. Due to this phenomenon, the Web information is reflecting current events and trends that are happening in the real world which, in turn, has attracted a lot of interest in using the Web as a tool for sociological, marketing, and survey research. For example, brand popularity and penetration may be observed from the Web using a simple technique such as plotting the number of occurrences of topical keywords (e.g. the brand names) in web pages over time.

In this paper, we will study the characteristics of *socio-topical web keywords*. The socio-topical web keyword, extracted from the content of some web pages, is a keyword relating to some topics of interest in a real-world society. The characteristics found in this study should provide some insights into the development of techniques and tools for detecting the emerging topics, and social trends from the Web.

We study the characteristics of socio-topical web keywords sampled from a series of Thai web snapshots. The Thai web snapshots were created by periodically crawling a subset of the Thai Web (we use the word "Thai Web" to represent a set of all web pages written in the Thai language that are accessible on the Web via some URLs). The series of Thai web snapshots consists of three dataset crawled on October 2006, December 2006, and January 2007.

The study was conducted as follows. First, the socio-topical keywords were sampled from the inverted index of each Thai web snapshot. Then, for each sampled keyword, we observe the pattern of changes of the number of documents containing the keyword, and the inverse document frequency (IDF) scores. Finally, we try to find the relationships between the observed patterns of changes and their corresponding real-world events in the Thai society by considering some examples of the socio-topical keywords extracted from the datasets.

The rest of the paper is organized as follows. In Section 2, we review some related works on the study of web evolution. Section 3 explains related basic concepts. Next, Section 4 describes our experimental environment and reports the results of our study. Finally, Section 5 concludes the paper.

2. Related Works

Much research has been done on detecting the emerging trends on the Web based on link analysis ([3, 4, 5,]). In [3], Amitay *et al.* proposed a time-stamped links based trend detection method. The time stamp of each link is determined from the Last-Modified time of the corresponding web pages. For a given keyword, they collected top pages of search results and pages that pointed to the top pages. Then, they plotted a histogram of time-stamped links for these set of pages to check the trend of the given keyword.

In September 2003, the Internet Archive [1] started providing a text search engine service (Recall [2]) over its 11 billion archived web pages. The Recall search engine offered time-based search and provided a graph showing changes of the frequency of the search query keyword over time along with the list of relevant results. The emerging and fading of the search query keyword may be determined from that graph. This time-based search service, which was once provided by the Internet Archive, represents an example of works on content-based trend detection from Web data.

3. Background

3.1. *Language Identification of Web Pages*

TextCat [7] is an implementation of an n-gram based text classification proposed by Cavnar and Trenkle [8]. In short, the concept of n-gram based text classification technique is to calculate a profile of an input document with an unknown category. Then, based on a comparison metric (such as an out-of-place metric) the profile of the input document will be compared with the profiles of all known categories which were created earlier using a number of documents of which the categories are known. The output of the classification is the name of the categories with the closest matches.

The n-gram based text classification technique can be easily applied to the task of language identification of web pages. In this context, any category can be viewed as corresponding to a language; a category's profile is used to represent a profile of a language. And, the classification output is the name of the languages with the closest matches.

In this research, we will use TextCat to identify the languages of crawled web pages. The TextCat library [7] comes with several built-in language profiles. Because our main concern here is to precisely identify the Thai web pages, the TextCat library has to be configured so that the precision of Thai web pages identification is maximized. This may be done, for example, by eliminating from the TextCat library some profiles of languages that are rarely found in the input data to reduce false positive classification of Thai web pages. In our experiment, we have eliminated some minority language profiles such as Welsh, Sanskrit, and Drents from the TextCat library.

Our language identification method can be described as follows.

(1) Remove all html tags from an input web page.

(2) A web page frequently includes English navigation menu, disclaimer, copyright texts, *etc.* at its top and bottom parts. These kinds of textual content can deteriorate the precision of the language classifier. To prevent the effects of such unrelated textual content on the classification

results, a portion of the first and the last parts of the resulting text from the previous step will be removed.

(3) Submit the remaining text from (2) to TextCat.

(4) If the output string of TextCat is UNKNOWN, then try to infer the language from the charset specified in html META tag. The input web page with html charset equals to "tis-620" or "windows-874" will be classified as a Thai web page.

(5) If the output string of TextCat contains [thai], the input web page will be classified as a Thai web page. Otherwise, the input web page will be classified as a non-Thai web page.

3.2. *Inverse Document Frequency (IDF score)*

An inverse document frequency (IDF score) is a measure of the general importance of the term. The IDF score is widely used in the TF*IDF weighting scheme to scale down the effects of terms that occur in many documents irrespective of the content. The intuition behind the IDF is that a term which occurs in many documents should be given less weight than one which occurs in few documents because it has less discrimination power.

The IDF score of a term t may be calculated by:

$$\text{IDF\_SCORE}(t) = 1 + \log(D/D_+) \tag{1}$$

where, D : is the total number of documents in the collection, and
D_+ : is the number of documents containing term t.

4. Experiments and Results

4.1. *Datasets*

In this section, we will describe a procedure for constructing the datasets used in our experiment. Firstly, a series of Thai web snapshots was first created by periodically crawling of Thai web pages. In order to selectively collect Thai web pages from the World Wide Web, we have applied a language specific web crawling strategy as proposed in [6] and [11]. In all of the crawls, the start URLs used are: http://webindex.sanook.com/ and http://directory.truehits.net/ (both URLs are the homepages of Thai web directories). The crawls were conducted consecutively in October 2006, December 2006, and January 2007. Then, for each Thai web snapshot, only the Thai web pages were selected and added into the dataset. The number of Thai web pages in each dataset is shown in Table 1.

Table 1. Number of Thai web pages and number of distinct keywords in each dataset.

Dataset	Crawl Period	Number of Thai web pages	Number of distinct keywords
Thai200610	October 2006	210,889	1,611,055
Thai200612	December 2006	108,415	1,046,739
Thai200701	January 2007	280,429	2,074,516

Note that, a Thai web page is a web page that is likely to be written in Thai language. The language identification of web pages was done using the method explained earlier in Section 3.1.

4.2. *Experimental Setup*

In order to study the characteristics of the socio-topical web keywords in the datasets, it is necessary to tokenize textual content of all web pages in the datasets and create inverted indexes which store statistics about the tokens found in the documents. In the following subsections, we will discuss about the tokenization of Thai web pages and the creation of the inverted indexes.

4.2.1. *Tokenization of Thai web pages*

Tokenization refers to the process of converting textual content of the documents into a stream of words which will later be used as the index terms in an inverted index [13, 12].

In Thai written text, there is no word boundary. Thai words are implicitly recognized based on judgment of individual reader. There are many works on word segmentation problem for Thai language *e.g.* [14, 15 and 16]. In this paper, the tokenization of textual content of Thai web pages was done using the ThaiAnalyzer [10], which is a software package providing Java APIs for tokenizing Thai text.

4.2.2. *Creation of the Inverted indexes*

An inverted index [17] is a data structure that maps terms to the documents that contain them. The inverted index is widely used to allow full text search on a collection of documents. In our experiment, we will use the inverted indexes of the Thai datasets to extract socio-topical web keywords.

The Apache Lucene API [9] is an open-source text search engine library written entirely in Java. In Lucene, the inverted index maps terms to documents containing it. In order to make term-based search more efficient, The Lucene's index also stores statistics about terms, such as term frequency and the number of documents containing the terms.

We have created inverted index for each dataset using Apache Lucene API. The number of distinct keywords (*i.e.* terms) in the resulting inverted index for each dataset is as shown in Table 1.

4.3. Results: Characteristics of Some Socio-topical Web Keywords

As the first step toward the extraction of important topical keywords from a series of web snapshots, in this paper, we will study the characteristics of such keywords from our Thai web snapshots. We have selected some topical keywords to study their characteristics (see Table 2). In the selection of these keywords, we have tried to choose the keywords that are related to events in the real world according to the crawl time of the web snapshot. For example, the first keyword "ปฏิวัติ" (coup) has been selected as an interesting keyword because during the end of September 2006, there was a coup in Thailand.

4.3.1. The number of documents containing the socio-topical keywords

Let us now consider the number of documents containing the keywords (D_+). From Table 2, it can be seen that the D_+ value is increasing when the corresponding real-world event is approaching or when the corresponding topic is gaining more interest from the society. For example, in the case of socio-topical keyword "New Year", it can be seen that its D_+ value is increasing sharply when the "New Year" is approaching (*i.e.* from 273 in December 2006 to 1772 in January 2007).

4.3.2. IDF scores of the socio-topical keywords

The IDF score of each keyword in the inverted indexes was calculated using Equation (1). The range of the IDF scores for the keywords in our dataset is from 1.0 to 12.0. Table 2 shows the IDF scores of some selected socio-topical web keywords in our Thai dataset.

According to our observation, the IDF scores of the keywords that are related to the real-world events are mostly in the middle part (*i.e.* 3.5 to 6.5) of the IDF scores ranking. From Table 2, the IDF scores of all keywords do not significantly vary over time.

Table 2. IDF scores and D_+ of some socio-topical web keywords.

Keyword (meaning)	IDF scores (Number of documents containing keywords; D_+)		
	Thai2006210	Thai200612	Thai200701
ขึ้นปีใหม่ (New Year)	8.01 (190)	6.98 (273)	6.06 (1772)
ปฏิวัติ (Coup)	5.96 (1476)	6.29 (545)	6.21 (1517)
ทักษิณ (Name of a former Prime Minister of Thailand)	4.58 (5705)	4.78 (2448)	5.22 (4091)

The observations from the study of the characteristics of the socio-topical keywords in Section 4.3.1 and 4.3.2 are as follows.

- The evolution of the number of documents containing the selected socio-topical web keywords (D_+) correctly reflects the trends of corresponding real-world events.
- The evolution of the IDF scores of the selected socio-topical web keyword does not significantly reflect changes in the real-world.
- However, based on the observation that the socio-topical web keywords typically have IDF scores within the range of 3.5 to 6.5, it may be possible to use the IDF scores for automatically discriminating or determining the socio-topical keywords out of a large number of keywords in the inverted indexes of the datasets.

5. Conclusions and Future Works

The popularity of the Web as a medium for disseminating information, news, ideas, and opinions of the modern society has attracted a lot of interest in using it as a tool for observing and understanding emerging social trends, ideas, and opinions. To facilitate this kind of sociological research, we have conducted a preliminary study on the characteristics of socio-topical web keywords sampled from a series of Thai web snapshots.

Two attributes of each sampled socio-topical web keywords were investigated: (1) the number of documents containing the keywords, and (2) the inverse document frequency (IDF) scores of the keywords. According to our experimental results, we found that the evolution of the number of documents containing the socio-topical web keywords correctly reflects the trends of corresponding real-world events. We also found that a socio-topical web keyword typically has an IDF score within the range of 3.5 to 6.5.

As for the future works, we will evaluate and improve the quality of the inverted indexes produced by the ThaiAnalyzer package [10]. We also planned to crawl a larger number of Thai web pages more frequently.

References

1. Wayback Machine, *The Internet Archive.* http://www.archive.org/.
2. A. Patterson, *CobWeb Search.* http://ia00406.archive.org/cobwebsearch.ppt.
3. E. Amitay, D. Carmel, M. Herscovici, R. Lempel and A. Soffer, *Trend Detection through Temporal Link Analysis.* J. Am. Soc. Inf. Sci. Technol, **55(14)**, 1270-1281 (2004).
4. R. Kumar, J. Novak, P. Raghavan and A. Tomkins, *On the Bursty Evolution of Blogspace.* Proceedings of the 12th International Conference on World Wide Web, 568-576 (2003).
5. D. Gruhl, R. Guha, D. Liben-Nowell and A. Tomkins, *Information Diffusion through Blogspace.* Proceedings of the 13th International Conference on World Wide Web, 491-501 (2004).
6. K. Somboonviwat, T. Tamura and M. Kitsuregawa, *Finding Thai Web Pages in Foreign Web Spaces.* ICDE Workshops 2006, 135 (2006).
7. WiseGuys Internet B.V., *libTextCat – lightweight text categorization.* http://software.wise-guys.nl/libtextcat/.
8. William B. Cavnar and John M. Trenkle, *N-gram based text categorization.* Proceedings of SDAIR-94, 3rd Annual Symposium on Document Analysis and Information Retrieval, 161-175 (1994).
9. The Apache Software Foundation, *Apache Lucene.* http://lucene.apache.org/java/docs/index.html.
10. National Electronics and Computer Technology Center (NECTEC) Thailand, *ThaiAnalyzer Package.* http://sansarn.com/look/download.html.
11. K. Somboonviwat, T. Tamura and M. Kitsuregawa, *Simulation Study of Language Specific Web Crawling.* ICDE Workshops 2005, 1254 (2005).
12. Soumen Chakrabarti, *Mining the Web: Discovering Knowledge from Hypertext Data.* Morgan Kaufmann Publishers (2003).
13. R. Baeza-Yates and B. Ribeiro-Neto, *Modern Information Retrieval.* Addison Wesley Longman Limited (1999).
14. V. Sornlertlamvanich, T. Potipiti, C. Wutiwiwatchai, P. Mittrapiyanuruk, *The State of the Art in Thai Language Processing.* Proceedings of the 38th Annual Meeting on Association for Computational Linguistics, 1-2 (2000).

84

15. S. Meknavin, P. Charoenpornsawat and B. Kijsirikul, *Featured Based Thai Word Segmentation.* Proceedings of Natural Language Processing Pacific Rim Symposium, 41-46 (1997).
16. V. Sornlertlamvanich, T. Potipiti and T. Charoenporn, *Automatic corpus-based Thai word extraction with the c4.5 learning algorithm.* Proceedings of the 18th conference on Computational linguistics, **2**, 802-807 (2000).
17. J. Zobel and A. Moffat, *Inverted files for text search engines.* ACM Computing Surveys, **38(2)**, Article No. 6, (2006).
18. Sparck Jones, K. *A statistical interpretation of term specificity and its application in retrieval.* Journal of Documentation, **28**, 11–21 (1972).

DYNAMERGE: A MERGING ALGORITHM FOR STRUCTURED DATA INTEGRATION ON THE WEB

FRANÇOIS SCHARFFE

Digital Enterprise Research Institute,
Leopold-Franzens-Universität,
Innsbruck, Tyrol, Austria
Email: francois.scharffe@deri.org
http://www.deri.org

Integrating various data sources is a major problem in knowledge management. Integration systems proposed in the last two decades as a solution start showing some limitations for various reasons. First the environment scaled from a few data sources in the same location to an unknown number of possible data sources on the Web. Second the sources to be integrated may change quickly over time. We propose in this article a method allowing for the dynamic integration of data sources on the web. Based on a network of schemas (database schemas, ontologies) related via mappings our algorithm generates a global view over a set of resources. Our approach presents the advantage to minimize the necessary human intervention in order to integrate sources.

Keywords: Ontology Merging, Structured Data Integration, Web

1. Introduction

The integration of heterogeneous data sources has a long research history following the different evolutions of information systems. Different approaches have been studied from whose two general classes can be extracted. Federated systems [1–3] using a global schema and mappings between the source schemas an the global schema, and distributed systems [4,5] where peers are integrated using one-to-one mappings. The second approach, more recent, follows the emergence of the web and its extension towards a machine-processable, structured, semantic web [6]. While the federated approaches were adapted for the integration of a limited number of data sources in a close environment, they have started to show limitations in the open environment the web constitutes. Distributed approaches overcome these limitations by offering a scalable architecture.

There would be no problem if data sources where obeying a common schema. It is obviously not the case. Many different ontologies are describing various domains with possible intersections. The answer to the schema heterogeneity problem came early in the database integration field via the use of *mappings* and is still a hot topic in ontology research, particularly on automatic mapping, see [7,8] for recent surveys. The problem of automatically relating overlapping two ontologies is still open [9].

A potentially huge number of ontologies can be related via mappings. Multiple questions are raised at this level about the scalability of an ontology network or about the way to give a consistent and unified view over the data.

Scalability — In the case where we want to exchange data between a large number of sources each described by their own schema, those need to be related together. Integrated approaches where data sources where related to a hand-made global schema are no longer applicable in a scenario where tousands of schemas have to be related. A more *collaborative* approach is more likely to appear where schemas are related one-to-one or one-to-a-few by diverse entities, and the mapping published. In that perspective the complexity of the mapping network grows in $\Theta(n^2)$ of the number of schemas in it. Such a complexity is obviously not acceptable in an environment like the web.

Redundancy — As an information space integrates more and more previously mapped schemas, redundancy between the mappings begin to appear. The transitivity between mappings should be maximally exploited in order to reduce, or better suppress this redundancy. It only has for an effect to augment the length of paths between schemas in the mapping network, and therefore the number of data transformations and query rewriting steps to achieve proper data integration.

Mediator systems where developped as a way to integrate heterogeneous data source by providing a unified view over the data. They are as already argued not scalable in a wide, open environment. The main evolutions of this environment resides in the distributivity or resource repartition, as well as the increased number of possible integrated resources. Next section presents existing solutions for such an environment.

Inconcistencies — An important question is about solving the inconsistencies created by the alignment of many logical theories. [10] propose a framework to reason with inconsistent ontologies. Then come problems close to the ones that arisen in database integration, the fundamental question being how to provide an unified view of the information to a particular application or service. The obvious solution is to create a global ontology and relate it to domain specific schemas. This requires first to build a global schema capturing the concepts of the local schemas and second to draw the mappings between each local schemas to the global one. There is an extensive amount of work since 20 years on this topic [1–3,11,12]. The bottleneck has always been the necessary human intervention. It is still a problem as it is a time consuming task. Creating a new global schema and relating it to the local schema each time you want to define or redefine an application is not realistic in the context of the semantic web where services are expected to be dynamically created given some requirements.

Section 3 study the evolution of information systems, showing fundamental differences in the problem shape. We present the algorithms to construct the unified view in Section 3. Finally future work and conclusions are given Section 5.

2. Idea: Providing a Unified View

The classical information integration problem consists in finding a way to relate databases in order to provide a unified view over the data. Solutions emerged proposing the use of *mediators* [13] making the link between local schemas and the global hand-made schema.

The shape of the data integration problem however changed. The rising up of the web makes it nowadays possible to easily publish and access data across the world, resulting in a large number of available data sources. New formalisms and systems to describe and manage structured data arose as well. We can already identify two changes:

(1) The number of potentially available sources is much larger
(2) Different formalisms are used to describe data

Ontology mediation means to solve this problem by allowing to create mappings between ontologies. Two different approaches are proposed. The first approach consists in applying database integration research to the ontology work by using global ontologies which are related to domain ontologies or databases. This approach is however not likely as the mappings and the global schema must be designed from scratch for each application. Also the necessary human intervention considerably limit the dynamics of the process.

The second approach consists in linking ontologies one to one. Issues appear when trying to reason over this network of ontologies as first, inconsistencies appear and second the complexity of the network raises scalability problems. Besides this theoretical limitations, this approach doesn't provide a unified view over the data, which make querying more complex for the user. We believe a better solution to information integration can be brought. In order to get closer to this solution we detail in the following issues.arising when trying to integrate data on the web.

From this analysis we conclude the need to somehow fill the gap existing between centralized, "old school" data integration systems paradigm and to adapt it to the distributed, large scale environment of the web. This adaptation require some modifications in the way mappings and global schemas are designed.

We propose to dynamically generate a global ontology out of a set of ontologies related together with mappings. We study the feasibility of automatic generation of this global ontology and show the advantages of having a unified view over the data, reusing the mappings between ontologies, strongly reduce the complexity of the network and therefore augment the scalability of semantic web applications. Generating a global ontology from a set of ontologies is related to ontology merging and database schema integration. However, merging ontologies is always a semi automatic task as the mappings have first to be provided. Our approach concentrates on the automatic generation of the global ontology, *given* the mappings. We need a dynamic process where ontologies can be added or removed from network, thus modifying the global ontology.

We integrate structured data sources designed using various meta-languages. In order to achieve this we provide a way to create mappings in an abstract way from the meta-language used to describe these sources. We use the abstract mapping language defined in [14]. Based on this mappings we are able to automatically generate a unified view over a set of related ontologies.

3. Method: Generating the Unified View

Based on a set of ontologies and mappings between them we are able to generate the unified view automatically. We first define a merge operator able to merge two ontologies related via a mapping. The process incrementally adding ontologies to the unified view using the merge operator is then described. This process allows for dynamically adding sources. For space reasons we do not detail the algorithms here.

3.1. *A merge operator*

The basic element of the merge process is a merge operator, taking in input two schemas and a mapping between them, and returning a merged schema. The merged schema G get the result of merge that take as a parameter a source schema O_s, a target schema O_t and a mapping between the two schemas $Map_{s,t}$.

The merge operator has to merge classes, attributes and relations found in ontologies. It must preserve the hierarchy relation and must solve possible conflicts. This operation has also for task to name the nodes of the resulting schemas, this is done by giving a preferred schema.whose nodes labels will be kept. Merge takes into account the complex correspondences expressed in the mapping such as one-to-many correspondences or conditions on attributes values.

Merge can at this state be decomposed in three procedures $mergeClasses(root(O_s))$, *mergeAttributes* and *mergeRelations* which merge respectively classes, attributes and relations of the given schemas. Merging classes[a]) is done by traversing the preferred schema concept tree from the root node using a breadth-first algorithm. This permits the proper creation of the merged schema concept tree in a top-down fashion.

The procedure *getMappingAndMerge(Class c)*[b] is called in the process of merging classes in order to retrieve the mapping rule corresponding to the class it currently processes and creates a proper merged node. If no corresponding rule is found, the node is simply added as a child of the node in the class hierarchy of the merged schema corresponding to its parent in the source (preferred) schema.

The *getMappingAndMerge(Class c)* procedure finds rules in which the current class appears and adds a new class to the unified view together with the mappings between the unified view and the two merged schemas (lines 4,5,6). We can note the new node is only attached to the preferred schema parent class. We deliberately don't specify the semantics of $c \in rule$, meaning that a class is part of a mapping rule, as variations exist that are not considered for the moment. If the processed node appear in no mapping rule it is added at the right place in the class hierarchy together with the corresponding mapping rule.

---

[a]We did not include the algorithm here for space reasons. We provide it on internet at http://www.scharffe.fr/pub/swiis2007/algorithm1.jpg
[b]We did not include the algorithm here for space reasons. We provide it on internet at http://www.scharffe.fr/pub/swiis2007/algorithm2.jpg

This merge operator allows the construction of the merging process between an evolving set of ontologies. Next section details this process.

3.2. *Maintaining the unified view*

Creating the unified view consists in incrementally merging the set of given schemas. This set is organized in a graph whose nodes are schemas and edges mappings relating schemas. More precisely, a unified view will be created over a subgraph of such a graph using the nodes corresponding schemas to be integrated.

Definition 3.1. Let the *context graph* be a graph $C =< S_c, M_c >$ whose nodes S_c represent the schemas to be merged and there is an edge $m(a, b) \in M_c$ if there is a mapping between the schemas corresponding to the nodes a and b.

Definition 3.2. Let the *merge candidate graph* be a graph $G =< S_g, M_g/S_g \sqsubset S_c, M_g \sqsubset M_c >$

Integrating the schemas raises the following obvious requirement on the topology of the context graph.

Proposition 3.1. *Either there is a path in G between every two nodes $a, b \in G$ or there is a path between a and b in C.*

Proposition 3.1 indicates that if merge candidate graph is not connected, then context graph must be so. The proof is obvious as two schemas cannot be integrated if there is no mapping (even indirect) between them. This proposition leads us to the problem of composing mappings. When there is no direct mapping between two schemas but there is a path between their corresponding nodes in the context graph, it is necessary to compose mappings in order to create a direct edge between the two nodes. Composing mappings is studied in databases [15], we plan to study the applicability of such methods to ontological schemas in future work (see Section 5).

Supposing the existence of a *Compose* operator, we are able to preprocess the merge candidate graph in order to add missing mappings using the composition operator. We obtain an extended merge candidate graph which is now connected.

Definition 3.3. Let *extended merge candidate graph* be a graph $G^{ext} =< S_{g_{ext}}, Mg_{ext}/S_{g_{ext}} = S_g, Mg_{ext} = M_g \cup M_{compose} >$ where $M_{compose}$ represents the set of mappings resulting of the *Compose* operator applied on disconnected components of the merge candidate graph.

The merge operator defined above take a preferred schema in order to solve naming and possible conflicts. We choose this preferred schema with the goal of minimizing the need of composing mappings. This leads us to give an order in which the unified view is created using merge. We make the assumption that the most *central* nodes in the merge candidate graph should be merged first, the process iterating with lesser central nodes, the growing unified view being always the preferred schema. We measure the *betweenness* of each nodes (see for example the definition in [16]) in order to determine its centrality in the ontologies network[c].

We suppose that there is always a mapping between the unified view and the schema to be merged. In practice this mapping has to be deduced from the schema already in the unified view whose corresponding node in the extended merge candidate graph is a neighbor of the node representing the schema to be merged. It can be easily proven that using a centrality ordering and having a connected graph, less central nodes will always be linked to a node which schema has previously been integrated in the central view.

A few work are dealing with automatically merging schemas. We review them in the next section.

4. Related Work

Most of the work on schema merging has been realized on semi-automatic merging. The first significant work in this area has been realized by C. Batini and M. Lenzerini *et al* in [11]. They present a comparative study on methods to merge database schemas and thus identify a number of criterion categorizing these methods. They particularly identify the inputs and outputs of the merging process and present the integration process cycle as:

Comparison of the schemas Corresponds to the process of mapping schemas.
Conforming the schemas Possible conflicts are solved during this phase
Merging and restructuring The proper merge of the schemas. Quality of the merge operation can be measured on the criteria of *completeness*, *correctness*, *minimality* and *understandability*.

---

[c]We did not include the algorithm here for space reasons. We provide it on internet at http://www.scharffe.fr/pub/swiis2007/algorithm3.jpg

This works give as well a taxonomy of the different integration strategies encountered. This review, giving the bases for database schema integration doesn't deal with automation of the process. It also considers database schemas and thus doesn't take into account hierarchical structures.

The mapping of the mappings to logical rules is an important part of the implementation studied in the data integration field. Local-as-view, Global-as-view approaches and their derivatives [1,12] provide techniques for writing the mapping rules by considering the global schema in terms of the local schemas or the other way around. More recently such techniques have been adapted for ontology integration, considering more expressive formalisms like description logics [17].

More recent research involving the merging of ontologies is presented by N. Noy *et al* and M. Musen in [18]. They propose a tool named PROMPT that helps to iteratively merge two ontologies based on suggestions from an algorithm. Most of the work is concentrated on the suggestion algorithm using linguistic and graph matching techniques to propose merge candidates. Based on the user choices, PROMPT proposes a set of operations which outcome is a new set of suggestions. The process guide the user in completely merging two ontologies. It also include some conflict resolution functionalities if entities are duplicated or dangling. Despite the popularity of this tool as being performant on merging ontologies, it is of medium relevance for our algorithm focuses on an automatic process, where mappings are already given.

In the RONDO system [19] S. Melnik and E.Rahm and P. Bernstein present an actual merge algorithm which input is as our algorithm taking two schemas and a mapping between them. The algorithm consists in three steps: node renaming, graph union and conflict resolution. The last step is let to be solved to the human engineerIn order to facilitate the conflict resolution procedure, the algorithm tags the merged nodes with a priority measure relating a preference over them. This algorithm only deals with equivalence, one-top-one mapping rules.

A more theoretical work is presented by P. Buneman, S. Davidson and A. Kosky in [20]. They study the merge operation and present a general technique to merge data models. Data models are first translated in a direct graph which nodes are classes and arcs relations or attributes of our model[d]. They consider merge as being a *commutative* and *associative* operation, so that schemas can be iteratively merge in any order. They distin-

---

[d]Including the meta relations Sub- and Super-.

guish between upper merge and lower merge operations which respectively return the least upper bound and the greatest lower bound of a collection of schemas in terms of information ordering.

Finally, in her PhD thesis [21], R. Pottinger considers a generic merge operator, as well as an merging algorithm. Her approach deals with complex mapping representation as a third party schema. She introduce the notion of *preferred model* for conflicts resolution. The merge operator defined is commutative and associative, as defined in [11]. This work is the closest we found to ours. The dynamic aspects of the merge operation are however not being taken into account[e].

5. Conclusions and Future Work

We have presented the evolution of the the information integration problem for structured data sources. From a closed word with a known, mostly static number of sources it evolved with the apparition of the web towards a dynamic environment. From a network of interelated ontologies we propose the automatic generation and maintenance of a unified view. This approach presents the advantages for the user to only have to query one schema. It also reduces the complexity of the necessary process of translating queries between the sources in the network. Our future work will concentrate on exploiting more complex mappings between the ontology entities. We will also study how mappings transitivity can be used to reach new sources.

References

1. M. R. Genesereth, A. M. Keller and O. Duschka, Infomaster: An information integration system, in *Proceedings of 1997 ACM SIGMOD Conference*, 1997.
2. D. Beneventano and S. Bergamaschi, The momis methodology for integrating heterogeneous data sources, in *IFIP World Computer Congress* (Toulouse, France, 2004).
3. G. Wiederhold, *Computer* **25**, 38 (1992).
4. A. Loeser, W. Siberski, M. Wolpers and W. Nejdl, Information integration in schema-based peer-to-peer networks, in *Proceedings of the Conference on Advanced Information Systems Engineering*, June 2003.
5. L. Predoiu, F. Martin-Recuerda, A. Polleres, C. Feier, A. Mocan, J. de Bruijn, F. Porto, D. Foxvog and K. Zimmermann, *Framework for Representing Ontology Networks with Mappings that Deal with Conflicting and Complementary Concept Definitions*, tech. rep., DIP EU project, FP6 - 507483 (2004).
6. B.-L. T., J. Hendler and O. Lassila, *Scientific American* (2001).

---

[e]In the related experiment it takes 20 hours to merge two big medical taxonomies.

7. P. Shvaiko and J. Euzenat, *A Survey of Schema-based Matching Approaches*, Tech. Rep. DIT-04-087, University of Trento (2004).

8. E. Rahm and P. A. Bernstein, *VLDB Journal: Very Large Data Bases* **10**, 334 (2001).

9. A. Halevy, *ACM Queue* **3**, 50 (2005).

10. Z. Huang, F. van Harmelen and A. ten Teije, Reasoning with inconsistent ontologies, in *Proceedings of the Nineteenth International Joint Conference on Artificial Intelligence (IJCAI'05)*, (Edinburgh, Scotland, 2005).

11. C. Batini, M. Lenzerini and S. B. Navathe, *ACM Comput. Surv.* **18**, 323 (1986).

12. M. Lenzerini, Data integration: a theoretical perspective, in *PODS '02: Proceedings of the Twenty-First ACM SIGMOD-SIGACT-SIGART Symposium on Principles of Database Systems* (ACM Press, New York, NY, USA, 2002).

13. G. Wiederhold and M. Genesereth, *IEEE Expert: Intelligent Systems and Their Applications* **12**, 38 (1997).

14. J. Euzenat, F. Scharffe and L. Serafini, *Specification of the Alignment Format*, tech. rep., Knowledge Web European Project (2006).

15. R. Fagin, P. G. Kolaitis, L. Popa and W.-C. Tan, *ACM Trans. Database Syst.* **30**, 994 (2005).

16. Betweeness definition in wikipedia `http://en.wikipedia.org/wiki/Betweenness`.

17. D. Calvanese, G. D. Giacomo and M. Lenzerini, A framework for ontology integration, in *Proc. of the First Semantic Web Working Symposium*, 2001.

18. N. F. Noy and M. A. Musen, Prompt: Algorithm and tool for automated ontology merging and alignment, in *Proceedings of the Seventeenth National Conference on Artificial Intelligence and Twelfth Conference on Innovative Applications of Artificial Intelligence* (AAAI Press/The MIT Press, 2000).

19. S. Melnik, E. Rahm and P. A. Bernstein, Rondo: A programming platform for generic model, in *Proceedings of SIGMOD 03*, 2003.

20. P. Buneman, S. B. Davidson and A. Kosky, Theoretical aspects of schema merging, in *EDBT '92: Proceedings of the 3rd International Conference on Extending Database Technology* (Springer-Verlag, London, UK, 1992).

21. R. Pottinger, Merging schemas and processing queries in support of data integration, PhD thesis, University of Washington, 2004.

INTEGRATION OF XML DATA SOURCES WITH STRUCTURAL DIFFERENCES

DIMITRI THEODORATOS and XIAOYING WU

Department of Computer Science,
New Jersey Institute of Technology,
E-mail: dth@njit.edu,xw43@njit.edu

A challenging issue in web is the integration of XML data sources. In this paper we address this issue when the XML data sources conform to schemas. This is a challenging problem because the XML documents may have significant structural differences even if they represent data from the same knowledge domain. We deal with it by (a) adding semantic information to the document schemas that allows the grouping of schema elements into the so called schema dimensions, and (b)using a query language that allows a partial specification of tree patterns. We show how the schema dimensions can form a dimension graph for all the data sources that acts as a global schema. Users posing their queries on this global schema have the flexibility of specifing structural constraints fully, partially or not at all. Our approach allows querying data sources with different schemas in an integrated way. We show how these queries can be translated into sets of branching paths expressions to be evaluated on the XML documents of the data sources. Our approach can be easily implemented on top of an XQuery engine.

1. Introduction

XML has emerged as the new language for representing and exchanging data on the web. XML models data in a tree-structured form. Often, XML documents of a certain application domain conform to schemas (DTD and more recently XML Schema[1]) that describe their structure. Existing languages for querying XML data rely on branching path expressions. These expressions specify tree patterns to be matched against the tree-structured XML data. XPath[1] implements branching path expression navigation in XML documents and lies at the core of XQuery,[1] the W3C proposal for querying XML documents.

The problem. A central issue in web integration is the querying of distributed data sources in an integrated way. This is a challenging issue. When integrating data sources, their structures have to be taken into account. When the data sources are XML data sources, additional complexity is introduced because the structure of the trees may be totally different. Data sources that conform to schemas may also have their schemas structured differently. Even if the data sources contain data from the same application domain and conform to the same schema, they may not have identical data structures because of the presence of optional elements.

A traditional virtual (or mediated[14]) approach to data integration creates a global schema. It then establishes mappings between this global schema and the schemas of the data sources that allow the translation of queries on the global schema to queries on the local schemas. In the case of tree structured data sources mapping rules need to be generated that translate subtree specifi cations on the global structure to subtree specifi cations on the local structures[5] This approach requires extensive manual effort and is error prone since all the mapping rules need to be correctly identifi ed in advance and hardcoded in the integration appli-cation. Query relaxation techniques[2] can also be used in an environment involving multiple data sources: the structural constraints of a query formulated on one local data source can be relaxed when the query fails to retrieve enough answers from another data source. Nevertheless, such techniques return approximate and not ex-act answers. Keyword search based approaches[9] can be used to query data sources with differences in their tree structures. However, the user does not have the pos-sibility to exclude answers that do not satisfy required structural constraints. In conclusion, existing approaches fail to provide satisfactory solutions to the prob-lem of integrating XML data sources with structural differences.

Contribution. In this paper we address the problem of integrating XML data sources that conform to schemas and have structural differences. We deal with it by (a) adding semantic information to the document schemas that allows the grouping of schema elements into the so called schema dimensions, and (b) using a query language that allows a partial specifi cation of tree patterns. The schema dimensions act as a new schema for querying. Users can formulate queries by specifying structural constraints between schema dimensions fully, partially or not at all. To evaluate partially specifi ed tree-pattern queries we defi ne the con-cept of schema dimension graph that abstracts the structural information of the schema of an XML document. Schema dimension graphs can be used to guide users in formulating queries, and to identify unsatisfi able queries. More impor-tantly, they allow the computation of a set of (completely specifi ed) tree pattern queries that together can compute the answer of a partially specifi ed tree-pattern query. These tree pattern queries along with schema dimension defi nitions are used to generate XPath expressions to be evaluated on the XML documents. In order to integrate data sources we create a global schema dimension graph in a global site by merging the dimension graphs of the data sources. We then show how queries addressed to the global site can be processed fi rst at the global site and then at the data sources. Our approach can be easily implemented on top of an XQuery engine.

2. Related Work

There are many systems that support the integration of tree-structured data using a predefi ned global structure and mapping rules between this structure and the local structures of the sources.[6] In the area of tree structured data, the Xyleme system[5] exploits XML views to cope with the problem of integrating XML data sources. The Agora system[10] translates XQuery expressions over a given global XML schema to SQL queries on local data sources. In,[4] YAT queries are posed on a global schema, processed using mapping rules, and then evaluated in the data sources.

Schema-based descriptions have been suggested for semi-structured databases. Dataguides[7] are structural summaries for semistructured data, storing statistics about paths and nodes, and enabling query optimization. In,[3] graph schemas are introduced to formulate and optimize queries for semistructured data. These approaches are purely syntactic. In contrast to our approach, they do not exploit semantic information. Query formulation is strictly dependent on the knowledge of structural irregularities in tree-structured data. In our approach, queries are not restricted by the structure of data. A problem similar to the one addressed in this paper is studied in.[9] The suggested language does not directly allow the specifi cation of several nodes on a tree pattern path without specifying an order for these nodes. In[11] the concepts of dimension and dimension graph were introduced with different semantics: the dimensions partition values of tree structures data. Here, schema dimensions partition the nodes of a schema tree that represent the elements of the schema. A query language that allows partial specifi cation of tree-patterns was introduced in.[12] We have adapted here this language to querying schema dimensions and we show how queries can be evaluated using schema dimension graphs.

3. Data Model

In this section, we introduce schema dimensions and we show how schema dimension graphs can be built from the schema of an XML document.

3.1. *XML document schemas*

We consider XML documents that conform to schemas. We view an XML document as a tree whose nodes are elements or values. Values can only be leaf nodes, and an element can have at most one child value node.

The schema of an XML document such as DTD can be represented as a tree whose nodes are labeled by the elements of the schema and the edges denote element-subelement relationships. Fig. 1 shows a tree representation for a DTD schema of an XML document. The schema tree of another document that conveys similar information is shown in Fig. 2. Abbreviations for the names of the elements are shown in Fig. 3.

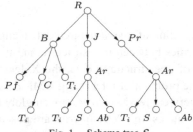

Fig. 1.   Schema tree S_1

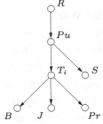

Fig. 2.   Schema tree S_2

3.2. Schema dimensions

The nodes of a schema tree may share common features. This semantic information allows the partitioning of the nodes into sets which are called *schema dimensions*. The semantic interpretation of the nodes is provided by the user, and may be different for different applications of the same data. A schema dimension may contain exactly all the nodes of the schema tree that are labeled by the same element. Alternatively, it may contain additional nodes, or nodes labeled by the same element may be assigned to different schema dimensions. Schema dimensions are assigned distinct names and thus are identifi ed with the sets of nodes they represent. By convention, every partition contains a set $\{R\}$ named R.

Consider the schema tree S_1 of Fig. 1. A trivial dimension set $\mathcal{D}_0$ of S_1 partitions together its nodes that have the same label. Fig. 4 shows another partition of the nodes of S_1 into a dimension set $\mathcal{D}_1$. The name of a set of nodes follows the $\rightarrow$. A partitioning of the nodes of the schema tree S_2 of Fig. 2 into a dimension set $\mathcal{D}_2$ is shown in Fig. 5.

The partitioning of the nodes of a schema tree S induces a partitioning of the element nodes (and their value nodes) of any XML document tree that complies with S. The partitioning approach allows us to deal only with the schema tree which is, in general, much smaller than its underlying XML document.

3.3. Schema dimension graphs

Based on a schema tree S and its dimension set $\mathcal{D}_S$, we can defi ne a schema dimension graph that summarizes S: the *schema dimension graph* of S and $\mathcal{D}_S$ is a directed graph $\mathcal{G} = (N, E)$, where: (a) the set of nodes N is the dimension set $\mathcal{D}_S$ of S, and (b) there is a directed edge in E from node D_i to node D_j iff a node of D_j is a child of a node of D_i in S. If $\mathcal{G}$ is the schema dimension graph of S, we say that S underlies $\mathcal{G}$.

Book	B		Title	Ti
JournalIssue	J		Preface	Pf
Proceedings	Pr		Abstract	Ab
Chapter	C		Article	Ar
Section	S		Publication	Pu

Fig. 3.   Abbreviations

$\{R\}$	$\rightarrow R$	
$\{B, J, Pr\}$	$\rightarrow Me$	$(Medium)$
$\{Pf, C, Ar\}$	$\rightarrow U$	$(Unit)$
$\{Ti\}$	$\rightarrow Ti$	
$\{S\}$	$\rightarrow S$	
$\{R/J/Ar/Ab\}$	$\rightarrow JAb$	$(Jour\_Abstract)$
$\{R/Pr/Ar/Ab\}$	$\rightarrow PAb$	$(Proc\_Abstract)$

$\{R\}$	$\rightarrow R$	
$\{P_u\}$	$\rightarrow U$	$(Unit)$
$\{Ti\}$	$\rightarrow Ti$	
$\{S\}$	$\rightarrow S$	
$\{B, J, Pr\}$	$\rightarrow Me$	$(Medium)$

Fig. 4. Partitioning of nodes of $\mathcal{S}_1$ into dimension set $\mathcal{D}_1$

Fig. 5. Partitioning of nodes of $\mathcal{S}_2$ into dimension set $\mathcal{D}_2$

Consider the schema dimension tree $\mathcal{S}_1$ of Fig. 1 and its dimension set $\mathcal{D}_1$ of Fig. 4. Fig. 6 shows the schema dimension graph $\mathcal{G}_1$ for $\mathcal{S}_1$ and $\mathcal{D}_1$. Fig. 6 also shows the schema dimension graph $\mathcal{G}_2$ for the schema dimension tree $\mathcal{S}_2$ of Fig. 2 and its dimension set $\mathcal{D}_2$ of Fig. 5.

A schema dimension graph of $\mathcal{S}$ and $\mathcal{D}_S$ abstracts the structural information of a schema $\mathcal{S}$ based on the semantic equivalences of nodes defined by the dimension set $\mathcal{D}_S$. As we will see later, schema dimension graphs are used (a) for guiding he user in formulating queries, (b) for checking queries for satisfiability, and (c) for supporting the evaluation of queries.

4. Query Language

In this section, we briefly present the query language. We define first partially specified tree-pattern queries and their answers and then we show how queries can be formulated on sets of schema dimensions.

4.1. *Queries on dimensions*

A query on a dimension set provides a (possibly partial) specification of a tree pattern. This tree pattern is to be matched against a document tree. A query specifies such a tree pattern through a set of *partially specified paths* (abbreviated *PSPs*) from the root of the tree. The edges of *PSPs* are precedence ($\Rightarrow$) or child ($\rightarrow$) relationships. A query also involves *node sharing expressions* denoted by an edge labeled by $\equiv$. One of the *PSPs* characterizes output *PSP*. We graphically represent queries using graph notation. Fig. 7 shows the graphical representations of two example queries whose semantics will be explained later.

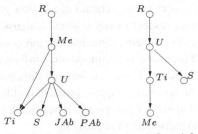

Fig. 6.   Schema dimension graph $\mathcal{G}_1$ and $\mathcal{G}_2$

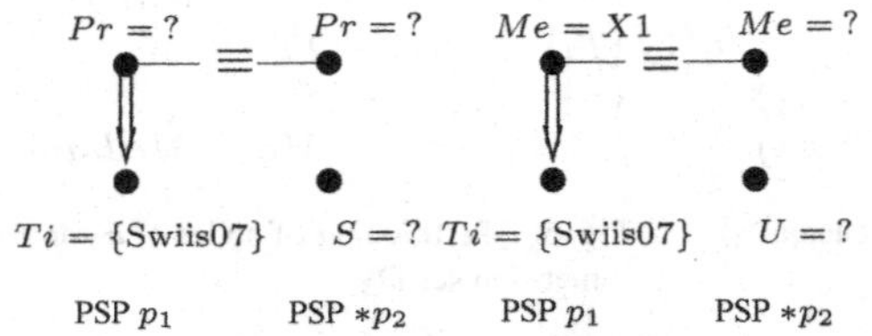

Fig. 7. Query Q_1 and Q_2

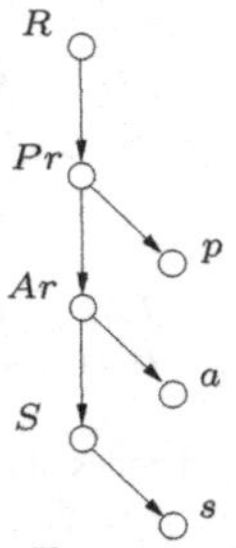

Fig. 8. Tree patterns in the answer of query Q_1

4.2. Query answers

Let T be an XML document that conforms to a schema S, and Q be a query on the dimension set $\mathcal{D}_S$ of S. An *embedding* of Q into T is a mapping m of the annotated dimensions of Q to the elements of T that preserves the PSPs, the annotations, the prec. Relationships and the node sharing expressions.

The embedding m induces a mapping from PSPs in Q to paths from the root of T. The *answer* of Q on T is the set of the images on the output *PSP* of Q under all the embeddings of Q in T.

Example 4.1. *Fig. 7 shows a query Q_1 on the trivial dimension set $\mathcal{D}_0$ of the schema tree S_1 of Fig. 1. Query Q_1 asks for a path involving elements Proceedings and Section such that element Proceedings has a descendant element Title whose value is "Swiis07". Notice that the query does not impose any order on Proceedings and Section: Proceedings can be a child or parent, ancestor or descendant of Section. Also, Proceedings, Title and Section can be in the same path, in which case, Section can be an ancestor or descendant of Title. The answer of Q_1 on an XML document T_1 that conforms to the DTD of Fig. 1 contains subtrees of T_1 whose pattern is shown in Fig. 8. Nodes p, a, and s are values and can be missing.* □

4.3. Query formulation

A query Q is called *unsatisfiabe with respect to a schema dimension graph $\mathcal{G}$* if and only if its answer is empty on every XML document that conforms to a schema underlying $\mathcal{G}$. For instance, it is not difficult to see that the query of Fig. 9 is unsatisfiable with respect to the schema dimension graph $\mathcal{G}_1$ of Fig. 6. In fact, it is unsatisfiable with respect to any schema dimension graph. An unsatisfiable query with respect to a schema dimension graph $\mathcal{G}$ can be detected by the system using only $\mathcal{G}$, and the user can be immediately informed possibly even during the formulation of the query. Therefore, schema dimension graphs can guide query formulation and can be used for query unsatisfiability checking. Unsatisfiable queries can also be defined with respect to schemas. We will elaborate further on unsatifiable queries in subsequent sections.

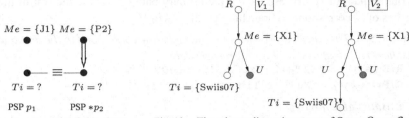

Fig. 9.   An unsatisfiable query   Fig. 10.   The schema dimensions trees of Query Q_2 on $\mathcal{G}_1$

5. Query Evaluation

We discuss in this section how queries on schema dimensions can be evaluated using schema dimension graphs.

5.1. Schema dimension trees

A partially specifi ed tree-pattern query can be evaluated by computing a set of (completely specifi ed) tree-pattern queries which are called *schema dimension trees*. Given a query Q and a schema dimension graph $\mathcal{G}$, a *schema dimension tree* of Q on $\mathcal{G}$ is a tree V whose root is labeled by the annotated dimension R, and its edges are child precedence relationships. It also has a distinguished node called *output node* that defi nes a path from its root called *output path*.

Intuitively, a dimension tree for Q on $\mathcal{G}$ represents an embedding of Q into $\mathcal{G}$ that respects labeling dimensions, precedence relationships, node sharing expressions and annotations (inclusively).

Example 5.1. *Fig. 7 shows a query Q_2 on the dimension set $\mathcal{D}_1$ of Fig. 4. The schema dimension trees V_1 and V_2 of query Q_2 on the schema dimension graph $\mathcal{G}_1$ of Fig. 6 is shown in Fig. 10. Black nodes denote the output nodes in the schema dimension trees. Question mark dimension annotations are omitted in the figures.*

5.2. Mapping schema dimension trees to XPath expressions

The schema dimension trees of a query Q on a schema dimension graph $\mathcal{G}$ are tree patterns that involve schema dimensions. In order to embed them to XML documents, schema dimensions need to be replaced by elements of a schema $\mathcal{S}$. The tree pattern queries that involve only elements of $\mathcal{S}$ are called *schema element trees* of Q on $\mathcal{S}$ and can be evaluated on an XML document. The answer of a schema dimension tree on an XML document T that conforms to a schema $\mathcal{S}$ is the union of the answers of its schema element trees on T.

Example 5.2. *Fig. 11 shows the element trees of query Q_2 on the schema tree $\mathcal{S}_1$ of Fig. 1. The first two are the schema element trees of the schema dimension tree V_1 while the other four are those of the schema dimension tree V_2 of Fig. 10.* □

Given a schema element tree W, an XPath expression e can be generated through a depth-fi rst traversal of W which traverses the output path of W last.

The output path of W corresponds to the primary path of e while the rest of the branches of U correspond to branching predicates in U.

Example 5.3. *The XPath expressions e_1 and e_6 below correspond to the first and last schema element trees of Fig. 11, respectively.*
$e_1 : R/B[\text{text}() = "X1"][Ti[\text{text}() = "Swiis07"]]/C$
$e_6 : R/Pr[\text{text}() = "X1"][Ar/Ti[\text{text}() = "Swiis07"]]/Ar$ $\square$

5.3. *Unsatisfiable queries*

In Subsection 4.3, we introduced the concept of unsatisfiable query with respect to a schema dimension graph. Detecting such an unsatisfiable query is useful mainly during the formulation of the query. Another notion of query unsatisfiability is more useful when evaluating a query: a query Q is called *unsatisfiabe with respect to a schema tree S* if and only if its answer is empty on every XML document that conforms to S. We can show the following proposition for checking query unsatisfiability with respect to a schema:

Proposition 5.1. Let D be the dimension set of a schema S, and Q be a query on D. Query Q is satisfiable with respect to S if and only if there is a schema element tree of Q on S. $\square$

Detecting an unsatisfiable query with respect to a schema is an important step in the evaluation of a query: it stops its computation at an early stage, before it reaches the XML document which are in general much larger than its schema.

6. Schema integration

We consider now different XML document data sources that comply with schemas and we show how they can be integrated. There are two major approaches to integrating data sources:[8] the materialized (or data warehousing)[13] and the virtual (or mediated).[14]

In this paper we follow a virtual approach. However, in contrast to a traditional virtual data integration approach, our approach does not require the creation and maintenance of schema mappings. We assume that a global set of schema dimension names N is fixed and used among the different data sources to be integrated. Each data source partitions its schema tree nodes and names the node sets with names from N. It also creates its schema dimension graph. In addition, a new

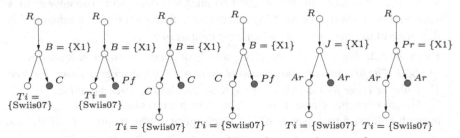

Fig. 11. The schema element trees of Query Q_2 on the schema tree S_1

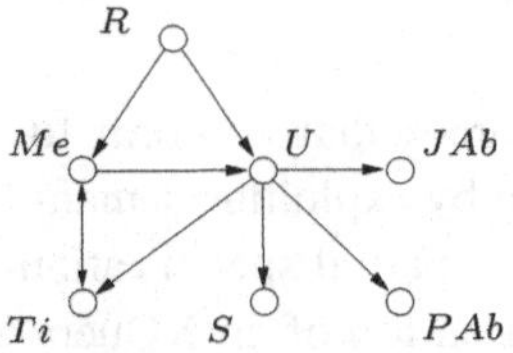

Fig. 12. Global schema dimension graph $\mathcal{G}$.

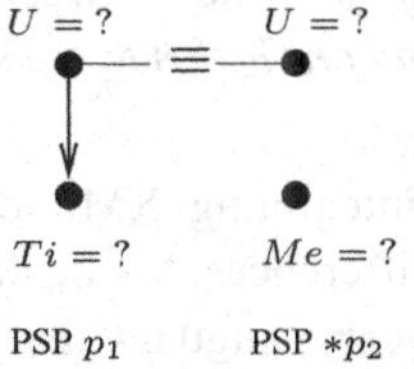

Fig. 13. Query Q_4

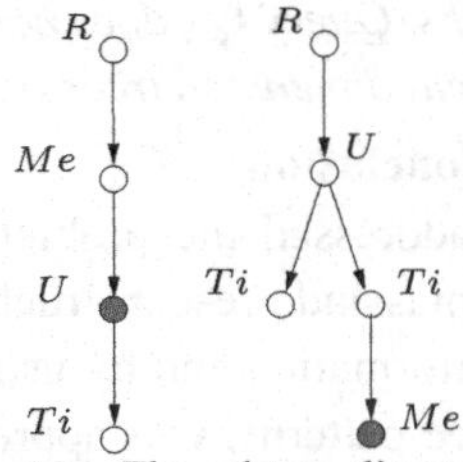

Fig. 14. The schema dimensions trees of Q_4 on $\mathcal{G}_1$ and $\mathcal{G}_2$

schema dimension graph is created that integrates the dimension graphs of the different data sources. We qualify this new dimension graph as *global*, as opposed to the dimension graphs of the sources which are characterized as *local*. The global dimension graph is used to guide user query formulation and to identify queries that are globally unsatisfiable (that is, unsatisfiable with respect to the global schema dimension graph).

6.1. *Global schema dimension graphs*

The global schema dimension graph is constructed by merging the nodes and edges of local schema dimension graphs.

Example 6.1. *Consider the schema dimension graphs $\mathcal{G}_1$ and $\mathcal{G}_2$ of Figures 6. Let's assume that these are the local schema dimension graphs of two sources. Fig. 12 shows the global schema dimension graph $\mathcal{G}$ for $\mathcal{G}_1$ and $\mathcal{G}_2$.*

6.2. *Query evaluation in an integrated system*

A query issued against an integrated system is specified on the global set of schema dimensions. Its answer is the collection of its answers on every local data source. The query is addressed to a global site that also stores the global schema dimension graph $\mathcal{G}$. Graph $\mathcal{G}$ guides the formulation of the queries. The system detects (and rejects) queries that are unsatisfiable with respect to $\mathcal{G}$. If a query is unsatisfiable with respect to $\mathcal{G}$ it is unsatisfiable with respect to the schema dimension graphs of all the data sources. The opposite is not necessarily true. Satisfiable queries are forwarded to the data sources where they are evaluated as described in Section 5, and their answers are sent back to the user. Since the query language allows partial specification of the structure, the same query can retrieve data from XML documents that conform to different schemas and have structural differences and irregularities.

Example 6.2. *Fig. 13 shows a query Q_4 on the global dimension set of the global schema dimension graphs $\mathcal{G}$ of Fig. 12. Even though the schema dimension graphs $\mathcal{G}_1$ and $\mathcal{G}_2$ summarize different structures, query Q_4 can retrieve data from XML documents conforming to schemas that underlie each of these schema dimension* *graphs. Query Q_4 does not specify an order between U and Me. Therefore, it has schema dimension trees on $\mathcal{G}_1$ and on $\mathcal{G}_2$. They are shown in Fig. 14.* $\square$

7. Conclusion

We addressed the problem of integrating XML data sources that conform to schemas and present structural differences. We dealt with it by exploiting semantic information and by using a query language that allows a partial specifi cation of tree patterns. Our approach can be easily implemented on top of an XQuery engine.

We are currently working on extending our approach so that it can take into account additional structural constraints that can be specifi ed on the schemas (e.g. uniqueness of a subelement, or mandatory subelements). We are also working on how to allow the user to query only a part (view) of the global dimension graph that is of interest to her.

References

1. World Wide Web Consortium site (W3C), http://www.w3c.org.
2. S. Amer-Yahia, S. Cho, and D. Srivastava, Tree pattern relaxation. In *Proceedings of the EDBT'02 Conference, Prague, Czech Republic*, 2002.
3. P. Buneman, S. B. Davidson, M. F. Fernandez, and D. Suciu, Adding structure to unstructured data. In *Proceeding of the ICDT'97 Conference*, Delphi, Greece, 1997.
4. V. Christophides, S. Cluet, and J. Simeon, On wrapping query languages and effi cient XML integration. In *Proc. of the ACM SIGMOD Conference*, 2000.
5. S. Cluet, P. Veltri, and D. Vodislav, Views in a large scale xml repository. In *Proc. of the Intl. Conference on Very Large Databases, Rome, Italy*, 2001.
6. H. Garcia-Molina, Y. Papakonstantinou, D. Quass, A. Rajaraman, Y. Sagiv, J. D. Ullman, V. Vassalos, and J. Widom, The TSIMMIS Approach to Mediation: Data Models and Languages, *Journal of Intelligent Information Systems*, 8(2):117–132, 1997.
7. R. Goldman and J. Widom, DataGuides: Enabling query formulation and optimization in semistructured databases. In *Proc. of the Intl. Conf. on Very large Databases*, 1997.
8. R. Hull and G. Zhou, A Framework for Supporting Data Integration Using the Materialized and Virtual Approaches. In *Proc. of the ACM SIGMOD Conference*, 1996.
9. Y. Li, C. Yu, and H. V. Jagadish, Schema-Free Xquery. In *Proc. of the 30th Intl. Conf. on Very Large Data Bases*, pages 72–83, 2004.
10. I. Manolescu, D. Florescu, and D. Kossmann, Answering xml queries over heterogeneous data sources. In *Proceedings of the VLDB Conference, Rome, Italy*, 2001.
11. D. Theodoratos and T. Dalamagas, Querying Tree Structured Data Using Dimension Graphs. In *Proc. of the Intl. Conf. on Adv. Information Systems Engineering*, 2005.
12. D. Theodoratos, T. Dalamagas, A. Koufopoulos, and N. Gehani, Semantic Querying of Tree-Structured Data Sources Using Partially Specifi ed Tree-Patterns. In *Proc. of the ACM Intl. Conf. on Information and Knowledge Management*, 2005.
13. D. Theodoratos and T. Sellis, Data Warehouse Confi guration. In *Proc. of the 23rd Intl. Conf. on Very Large Data Bases*, pages 126–135, 1997.
14. G. Wiederhold, Mediators in the Architecture of Future Information Systems. *Computer*, 25(3):38–49, 1992.

FUNCTIONAL DEPENDENCIES IN XML

XIANGGUO ZHAO, BIN WANG and BO NING

School of Information Science & Engineering, Northeastern University,
Shenyang, 110004, China

XML has become a standard for data representation and exchange on the Internet. The functional dependency is the most important part of the research on XML database normalization and there is already some research work on this topic. According to the types of existing complicated functional dependency constraint, the features of the data constraint are analyzed. A definition of XML functional dependency (XDF) is proposed which is based on a DTD path language. Compared with formal definitions already proposed, XFD proposed in this paper can express more XML dependencies, which makes it more suitable for further research work.

1. Introduction

Functional dependencies play an important role in integrity constraints and database designing, and this kind of data constraint mechanism plays an important role in management of XML data. To represent functional dependencies, relational database utilizes relational schema, while XML has its own schema, such as the*XML Data[1], XML Schema[2] and XML DTD[3]. But predefined semantic information is insufficient to represent functional dependencies. Data constraints of XML come from their semantics of application. Application constraints in XML data model is needed, by which the database can reject the processes that may cause inconsistence.

Many researchers are attempting to apply the concept of functional dependencies to XML data model. Based on the concept of tree-tuples, [4] proposes a definition of functional dependencies in XML (XFD), which treats DTD as a relational schema. Paths on the DTD are the attributes of the schema. [5] proposes an XFD based on the concept of closest node. Similar to the key defined in [6], closest node is the node mapped from the left side and the right side of the XFD in the XML tree, whose path instance has the maximum common prefix. [7] points out that the definitions in [4] and [5] are equal when there is no null values. [8] defines a local XFD. Similar to the way that relative key is defined in [6], it expresses data constraints on the XML fragments.

---

*This work is supported by National Natural Science Foundation of China under grant 60573089.

Considering hierarchical characteristic of XML database, [9] proposes a definition of functional dependencies (FDXML). [10] does some research in the logical implication and inference rules of XML key. [11] discusses definitions of previous XFD and proposes a general XFD (GXFDs). But only with the concept of GXFDs is worthless, since it lacks an effective axiom system[11]. To illustrate the ineffectiveness of the above definitions, see the example below:

Example 1: Figure 1 shows a DTD of an XML document about a school. There are many public courses and departments in school. Each department contains the information of a department name, a group of courses, some classrooms and some offices. A classroom includes room number and the number of buildings. An office includes office number, name and the number of buildings. Each course has a course number and a list of students that have registered the course. Student list is a group of students; each student has student ID and name.

```
<!ELEMENT school (course*, department*)>
<!ELEMENT course (slist*)>
  <!ATTLIST course cname CDATA #REQUIRED>
<!ELEMENT department
            (course*, office*, classroom*)>
  <!ATTLIST department
            dname CDATA #REQUIRED>
<!ELEMENT office (oname, addr)>
  <!ATTLIST office roomno CDATA #REQUIRED>
<!ELEMENT classroom (addr)>
  <!ATTLIST classroom
            roomno CDATA #REQUIRED>
<!ELEMENT slist (student*)>
<!ELEMENT student(sname )>
  <!ATTLIST student sno CDATA #REQUIRED>
```

Figure 1. The DTD about the school

We expect to express the following constraints on this DTD. In the whole document, a student number uniquely determines a student name; Course name uniquely determines the list of students; In the whole school, course name uniquely identifies a course and no course shares the same course name; In a department, office name determines the office number, but it is not applicable to the whole document; Department name determines the address of office and the classrooms (we assume that each department is in a specific building).

The above definitions of XFD except [11] are all based on the concept of paths in DTD, most of which only use the concept of simple path. Those definitions have expressed different kinds of data constraints respectively. As stated previously, there are more kinds of functional dependency constraints in XML data, however the approaches [4], [5], [8] and [9] XFD can not express these constraints, such as the following constraints: a), b), c), d) and e), [11] can not express e). Figure 2 shows a part XML of document about the information of a school.

```
<school>
  <course cname="c1">
    <slist>
      <student sno="s1"> <sname> Mary </sname> </student>
      <student sno="s2"> <sname> Joe </sname> </student>
    </slist>
  </course>
  <department dname="d1">
    <course cname="c2">
      <slist> <student sno="s1">
              <sname> Mary </sname>
              </student>
              <student sno="s3">
              <sname> Smith </sname>
              </student>
      </slist>
    </course>
    <office roomno="201">
      <oname> secretary </oname> <addr> build3-1 </addr>
    </office>
    <classroom roomno="301">
      <addr> build3-1 </addr> </classroom>
  </department>
</school>
```

Figure 2. An XML document about the school information

The above XML document is redundant, since the name *Mary* of student s1 and building number *build3-1* of department *d1* have to be stored twice. Such kind of redundancy will cause database anomaly[4]. Similar problem in relational database has been well solved by normalization theory, but not yet in XML database. Before studying XML normalization, we need to express those functional dependency constraints that will cause anomaly.

The contributions of our work are: 1). A new path language is proposed to navigate the nodes in XML documents by the vocabulary which can retrieve the node or node set in XML document. It is enough to express the functional dependencies, and it is simple. 2). A new method to express the functional dependencies is presented. It is able to express the functional dependencies which can cause the redundancy of data. 3). The functional dependencies which can cause the redundancy are summarized. With the compare of formal functional dependencies, the characteristics of our new method to express functional dependencies are concluded.

2. Symbol Definitions

2.1. *DTD and XML Document Tree*

Based on the definition in [4,6,7,11], a modified definition of DTD(document type definition) and XML tree are defined as follows:

Definition 1: DTD is a 6 tuple: $D = (E_c, E_s, A, F, R, r)$, where,

1) E_c is a finite set of complex element names;

2) E_s is a finite set of simple element names;

3) A is a finite set of attribute names;

4) F indicates a mapping from E_c to element type: for $\forall e \in E_c, F(e)$ is a regular string, $F(e) = \varepsilon \mid e' \mid (F(e) \mid F(e)) \mid F(e), F(e) \mid F(e)*$, where ε denotes null string, $e' \in E_c \cup E_s$ and "|",",","*" denotes union, join and Keleene closure respectively;

5) R indicates a mapping from E_c to attribute set; for $e \in E_c$,any $F(e)$ is not ε or $R(e)$ is not ϕ ;

6) $r \in E_c$ is a different element name, for $\forall e \in E_c$,r is the only one in E_c that does not exist in the alphabet of $F(e)$.

Note that the node types of XML document are divided into three types, complex element type, simple element type and attribute type. Simple element type does not contain child element type, complex element type can only be the element type but can not be defined as composite type, text only exists in attribute type and simple element type. XML DTD includes the definition of complex element, such as the definition of XFD in [4].The definitions in this paper will not lose semantic information of document and are easier to describe constraints.

Definition 2: XML Tree. An XML tree is usually defined to be $T = (V, lab, ele, att, val, tex, root)$, where,

1) V is a set of nodes in XML tree;

2) lab is a mapping from V to $E_c \cup E_s \cup A$, it returns the type of nodes in V; if $lab(v) \in E_c$, then a node $v \in V$ is called a complex element node; If $lab(v) \in E_s$, v is called a simple element node; If $lab(v) \in A$, v is called an attribute node;

3) ele and att are functions defined on complex element set: for every $v \in V$, if $lab(v) \in E_c$, then $ele(v)$ is a sequence of element nodes, and $att(v)$ is a set of attribute nodes with distinct labels;

4) val is a function that assigns a value to each attribute or element;

5) *tex* is a function that assigns a string value to each attribute or element, if $lab(v) \in E_c$, *tex(v)* is null; If $lab(v) \in E_s \cup A$, then *tex(v)* is the text contained by v;

6) *root* is a unique root node.

The XML document of school information in Figure 2 can be represented as Figure 3 according to the definition, and it is an XML tree that conforms to DTD in Example 1.

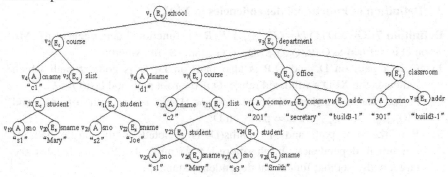

Figure 3. An XML document conforming the DTD

2.2. *Path Language*

Definition 3: Simple Path. Given a DTD D, a simple path is defined as $l_1 \cdots l_m$, where $l_i \in E_c$, $l_m \in E_c \cup E_s \cup A$ ($i < m$) is called a path step. l_i is in the alphabet $F(l_{i-1})$ for $i \in [2, m-1]$, and l_m is in the alphabet $F(l_{m-1})$ or in $R(l_{m-1})$.

Definition 4: Complex Path. A complex path defined as $l_1 \cdots l_n$, where $l_i \in E_c \cup \{/, //\}$, $i \in [1, n-1]$, $l_n \in E_c \cup E_s \cup A$, and at least one l_i exists so that $l_i \in \{/, //\}$. Symbol "/" is defined wildcard expressing one step in path, which can match any element or attribute, and symbol "//" represents the Kleene closure of the wildcard.

Definition 5: Matching Path. If $l_1 \cdots l_n \in$ Cpaths(D), where l_i is "/", $l_i \in E_c \cup E_s \cup A$, $l_1 \cdots l_{i-1}.l_i.l_{i+1} \cdots l_n$ is a simple path on D, then $l_1 \cdots l_{i-1}.l_i.l_{i+1} \cdots l_n$ matches $l_1 \cdots l_n$; if $l_1 \cdots l_n \in$ Cpaths(D), where l_i is //, P is a simple path on D, $l_1 \cdots l_{i-1}.P.l_{i+1} \cdots l_n$ is a simple path on D, then $l_1 \cdots l_{i-1}.P.l_{i+1} \cdots l_n$ matches $l_1 \cdots l_n$. A simple path that matches a complex path q is called the matching path of q. All the simple path that matches complex path q are defined as the matching set of q, denoted as {q}.

Definition 6: Path Instance. Let T be an XML tree conforming to D, v_0 be a node in T and P be a path in D, denoted as $l_1 \cdots l_n$. If the sequence of nodes in T $v_0.v_1 \cdots v_n$, $i \in [1, n]$ satisfies one of the followings:

a) If $l_i \in E_c \cup E_s \cup A \cup \{/\}$, v_i is the child of v_{i-1} and v_i matches l_i. Note that any node will match wildcard symbol "$/$";

b) If l_i is "$//$", ω represents any path instance on the subtree determined by v_0. If a path instance $v_1 \cdots v_{i-1}.\omega.v_{i+1} \cdots v_n$ exists, where $v_1 \cdots v_{i-1}$ matches $l_1 \cdots l_{i-1}$ and $v_{i+1} \cdots v_n$ matches $l_{i+1} \cdots l_n$, we call $v_1 \cdots v_n$ is a path instance of P with respect to v_0.

3. Definition of Functional dependencies in XML

Definition 7: Give DTD $D = (E_c, E_s, A, F, R, r)$, functional dependency in XML φ on D is defined as $O,(P,(Q_1,Q_2,...Q_n \rightarrow Q_{n+1}(S_1,...S_m)))$, where:

1) O is a path on D, and O.P is also path on D; O is context path which indicates the XFD's validated range. O is the root path and last(O)$\in E_c$.

2) P, Q_i for ($i \in [1, n+1]$), S_j for $j \in [1, m]$ is a path on D, and $P.Q_i$, $Q_{n+1}.S_j$, $P.Q_{n+1}$ are also paths on D;

3) P is the root path and $P \in$ paths(D) is denoted as the target path of functional dependency. Furthermore $P \neq \varepsilon$ (null), last(P)$\in E_c$ denotes the target nodes set that functional dependency stands;

4) $Q_1, Q_2, ..., Q_n$ are denoted as the left side path of φ, to express the determine factor of functional dependency, and Q_i for ($i \in [1, n]$) is a simple path on D, when Last(Q_i)$\in E_c \cup E_s \cup A$, and $Q_1, Q_2, ..., Q_n$ can not be ε at the same time;

5) Q_{n+1} is denoted as the right target path of φ, and $Q_{i+1} \in$ paths(D). Last(Q_i)$\in E_c \cup E_s \cup A$ are denoted as the range of functional dependency's right side;

6) $S_1, ... S_m$ are right side paths, which are simple paths, denote as the determine factor in XML tree. If $S_1, ..., S_m$ are all null paths, last(Q_{n+1}) is the determined-factor. If both Q_{n+1} and $S_1, ..., S_m$ are null path, last (P) is the determined-factor.

Semantic: for an XML tree T conforming to D, T satisfies XFDφ: $P,(Q_1,Q_2,...,Q_n \rightarrow Q_{n+1}(S_1,...,S_m))$. For any two nodes v_1 and v_2 of $[P.Qn+1]$, they are nodes in the subtrees with v_1' and v_2' in [P] as the root respectively, If $v_1'[Q_1], v_1'[Q_2],...,v_1'[Q_n]$ and $v_2'[Q_1], v_2'[Q_2],...,v_2'[Q_n]$ equal respectively, then $v_1'[S_1], v_1'[S_2],...,v_1'[S_m]$ and $v_2'[S_1], v_2'[S_2],...,v_2'[S_m]$ equal (or value equal) respectively.

We use " $\rightarrow$ " for value equality constraint and use " $\rightarrow_v$ " for equality constraint. Among the defined functional dependencies, most of them are expressing the dependency relationship between text values of nodes. Node equality is needed only when expressing the semantics of keys and no value equality of keys exiting in the target set. It is similar in the relational database that there are no 2-tuples with the key same values.

According to the definition of XFD, the data constraints in Example 1 can be represented as the following functional dependencies:

a) //.student,(@sno→(sname))

b) //.course,(@cno→(slist.student))

c) //.course,(@cno→$_v$ (ε))

d) school.department,(office,(oname→@roomno))

e) school.department,(@dno →/ (addr))

Note that if e) is replaced with another form.

f) school.department,(@dno →/ addr (ε))

Their semantics are different. "/" in e) is right target path, denoting the fifth constraint in Example 1, if the names of two department are value equal, then there building numbers are value equal too. For example, the XML document in Figure 3 satisfies constraints e). But the right target path in f) is /.addr and the right path is null, means that if the names of two departments are value equal, the building number sets of rooms owned by these two departments are value equal. When the right target path is null, the form school.department, (@dno →/ addr) is value equal with f).

XML Key[6] is a special case of XFD that we have proposed. Note that functional dependency c) expresses the semantic of key. @cno is a key of "course", which ensures entity integrity in document, and is defined as an absolute key in [6]. Meanwhile we can express relative key, such as on document fragment determined by department type of node in Example 1. @roomno determines an office type of node, i.e. an room number in a building can identify an office room. This kind of semantic is represented as functional dependency school.department,(office, (@roomno→$_v$ ε)).

4. Contrast Analysis of XFD

XFD proposed in this paper can express XML functional dependencies in [4], [5], [8] and [9]. We use the symbol XFD[i] to denote XFD in [i], and we express functional dependencies above with our XFD in this section. There are two examples in [4] that use the definition based on tree tuples of XFD[4] to express constraints.

One of the examples is a university database. This DTD satisfies three constraints, expressed by XFD[4] is presented below:

1) courses.course.@cno →courses.course

2) {courses.course,
    courses.course.taken_by.student.@sno}→courses.course.taken by.student

3) courses.course.taken_by.student.@sno →
   courses.course.taken_by.student.name.S
   it can be expressed by our XFD as the following:
1) courses.course,(@cno→$_v$ε)
2) courses.course,(taken_by.student,(@sno→$_v$ε))
3) courses.course.taken_by.student,(@sno→(name))

Another example is a document of DBLP, whose DTD satisfies four constraints: Distinct conferences have distinct titles. Articles of the same issue must have the same value in the attribute of year. For a given issue of a conference, distinct articles must have different titles. The key is an identifier for each article in the database.

These constraints are expressed by XFD $_{[4]}$ as the following:
1) db.conf.title.S → db.conf
2) db.conf.issue →db.conf.issue.inproceedings.@year
3) {db.conf.issue,
   db.conf.issue.inproceedings.title.S}→db.conf.issue.inproceedings
4) db.conf.issue.inproceedings.@key → db.conf.issue.inproceedings
   it can be expressed by our XFD as the following:
1) db.conf , (title →$_v$ε)
2) db.conf,(issue → issue.inproceedings(@year))
3) db.conf.issue,(inproceedings.title→$_v$inproceedings)
4) db.conf.issue.inproceedings,(@year →$_v$ε)

Since the expressing ability of the path language in XFD$_{[4]}$ is limited and it does not contain the concept of equal node values, it can not express the five constraints in Example 1 given in this paper. For example constraint a) can be expressed by XFD$_{[4]}$ as shown in the following two expressions
● school.department.course.slist.student.@sno→
  school.department.course.slist.student.sname.S
● school.course.slist.student.@sno→ school.course.slist.student.sname.S

They can only work on two parts of document respectively, instead of the whole document. For example, if the value of v25 in Figure 3 is changed to S2, the document satisfies the two constraints expressed by XFD[4], but it does not satisfy constraint a) in Example 1. Similarly XFD[4] can not express other constraints in Example 1 either.

Function dependencies in [5] are equal to that in [4] in case of ignoring null values. [13] extends the definition of functional dependencies (FDs) in incomplete relations to XML documents and makes a good research on problems relevant to null values in XML function dependencies. Problem of null value will not be discussed here.

XFD in [9] aimed at the hierarchical characteristic of database, and all of those can be expressed by XFD of this paper. These two constraints expressed by $XFD_{[9]}$ is presented below:
1) /PSJ/Project,[Supplier,Part → Price]
2) /PSJ,[Project,Supplier,Part → Quantity]

They are expressed by XFD of this paper as the following:
1) PSJ.Project.Supplier,(Part.@PartNo → Part.Price)
2) PSJ.Project,(Supplier.@SName,Supplier.Part.@PartNo→ Supplier.Part. Quantity)

Also the five constraints in Example 1 can not be expressed by $XFD_{[9]}$.

GXFDs in [11] have strong ability to express functional dependency, but its path language and concept of equality are complicated. It is hard to make the implication and inference problems clear. When function dependencies are used in integration constraints and normalizing theory, we simply need to choose those XML function constraints which are useful to these applications.

These constraints are expressed by $XFD_{[11]}$ as below:

1) _* .student: @sno → @sname

2) _* .student: @sno → address

3) _* .student: @sno → address(L)

4) _* .student.address : ⇑ .@sno → ε (S)

5) course.students.student.$text : ⇑ ^{3}→ ε (S)

6) _* .student : $tel(I) → address.

This paper does not consider the sequence of document and equality that intersection of sets is not null. We believe that it is not important for normalization theory of XML. The redundancy caused by constraint 3) can be expressed by constraint 2). Similar to constraint 6), redundancy caused by the fact that intersection of sets is not null can be replace by set equality. We can expand the concept of equality of ordered list and equality that intersection of sets is not null to our XFD, Constraints 1), 2), 4), 5) can be expressed by XFD of this paper as below:
1) //student,(@sno→ @sname)
2) //student,(@sno→ address)
4) //student,(@sno→ (address))
5) school. course,(@cno→ students.student(text))

Since its right side is a simple path whose length is 1 or 0, $XFD_{[11]}$ can not express constraint e) in Example 1.

5. Conclusion

This paper studies the problem of functional dependencies in XML, proposes a new method to represent XFD for expressing data constraints in XML that cause redundancy, points out the relationship between XFD and key (absolute key and relative key). This paper also summarizes the former work on functional dependencies in XML, analyzes their expressing formation and compares the expressing ability with XFD; XFD proposed in this paper can express more functional dependencies in XML document. There are two aspects for future work: one is reasoning and algorithm research based on XFD mentioned in this paper, the other is XML normalization.

References

1. Andrew Layman, Edward Jung, Eve Maler, and Henry S. Thompson, Xml-data. Technical report, *W3C Note*, http://www.w3.org/Tr/1998/Note-xml-data (1998).
2. Henry S. Thompson, David Beech, Murray Maloney, and Noah Mendelsohn, Xml schema part 1: Structures. Technical report, *W3C Recommendation*, http://www.w3.org/TR/xmlschema-1/ (2001).
3. ArborText Incl W3C XML specification DTD, *W3C Recommendation*, http://www.w3.org/XML/1998/06/xmlspec-report-199809101.htm (1998).
4. Arenas M. and Libkin L., A normal form for XML documents, *ACM Transactions on Database Systems*, pp. 195–232 (2004).
5. M. W. Vincent, J. Liu, and C. Liu, Strong functional dependencies and their application to normal forms in XML, *ACM Transactions on Database Systems*, pp. 445–462 (2004).
6. P. Buneman, S. B. Davidson, W. Fan, and C. S. Hara, Keys for XML. *In Proc. of Computer Networks*, pp. 473–487 (2002).
7. M. W. Vincent, J. Liu, C. Liu, and M. Mohania, On the definition of functional dependencies in XML, http://www.cis.unisa:edu.au/~cismwv/papers/index.html, (2005).
8. Jixue Liu, Millist Vincent, and Chengfei Liu, Local XML functional dependencies. *In Proc. of WIDM'*, pp. 23–28 (2003).
9. M. L. Lee, T. W. Ling, and W. L. Low, Designing functional dependencies for XML. *In Proc. of EDBT*, pp. 124–141 (2002).
10. Peter Buneman, Susan Davidson, Wenfei Fan, *et al.*, Reasoning about keys for XML. *In Proc. of Inf. Syst.*, pp. 133–148 (2001).
11. Junhu Wang, A Comparative Study of Functional Dependencies for XML. *In Proc. of APWeb*, pp. 308–319 (2005).
12. Wanfei Fan and Leonid Libkin, On XML integrity constraints in the presence of DTDs. *In Proc. of JACM*, pp. 368–406 (2002).

Author Index